cake keeper Cakes

100 Simple Recipes
for Extraordinary Bundt Cakes,
Pound Cakes, Snacking Cakes, and Other
Good-to-the-Last-Crumb Treats

LAUREN CHATTMAN

The Taunton Press

 The Taunton Press
Inspiration for hands-on living®

The Taunton Press, Inc.
63 South Main Street, PO Box 5506
Newtown, CT 06470-5506
e-mail: tp@taunton.com

Editor: Erica Sanders-Foege
Copy Editor: Betty Christiansen
Indexer: Heidi Blough
Jacket/Cover design: Teresa Fernandes
Interior design: Teresa Fernandes
Layout: David Giammattei
Photographer: Alexandra Grablewski

Library of Congress Cataloging-in-Publication Data

Chattman, Lauren.
  Cake keeper cakes : 100 simple recipes for extraordinary bundt
cakes, pound cakes, snacking cakes, and other good-to-the-last-
crumb treats / Lauren Chattman.
     p. cm.
  Includes index.
  ISBN 978-1-60085-120-9
1. Cake. I. Title.
TX771.C455 2009
641.8'653--dc22
                              2009021124

Printed in the United States of America
10 9 8 7 6 5 4 3 2 1

Acknowledgments

Thank you a million times to Erica Sanders-Foege for all of your extremely helpful advice and inspiring enthusiasm during every phase of this project. To everyone at Taunton who has been so supportive from beginning to end—Sue Roman, Don Linn, Teresa Fernandes, Betty Christiansen, Katy Binder, Sharon Zagata, Catherine Levy, Janel Noblin—thank you. I love working for Taunton because of all of you. Alex Grablewski's photos show exactly why you'd want to keep a cake on your countertop at all times. Thanks to Megan Schlow, Lynda Whyte, Tracy Keshani, and Todd Bonné for your work on these beautiful photos. A big thank you to Angela Miller, as always, for your help on this project specifically and for all of the support/cheerleading in general. And thanks again to Jack, Rose, and Eve for the cake keeper and the running commentary as I stocked it with a new cake every other day.

A former pastry chef, Lauren Chattman apprenticed under François Payard at Restaurant Daniel in New York and was the pastry chef at Nick and Toni's in Easthampton. She is the author of ten cookbooks and co-author of numerous other books, including *Dessert University* with former White House pastry chef Roland Mesnier and *Local Breads* and *Panini Express* with Daniel Leader. Her recipes have appeared in many national publications, including *Food & Wine, Bon Appetit, Cook's Illustrated, The New York Times,* and *Redbook.* She lives in Sag Harbor, New York, with her husband and two daughters.

22

32

66

TABLE OF
Contents

110

144

157

Introduction

There is a beautiful gourmet shop around the corner from my house where little cakes as well as breads, cheeses, and other enticing items are displayed under an array of antique glass domes. As soon as I saw those domes, I began to covet them. Last Mother's Day, my husband and children presented me with a beauty, and since then, it's been my mission to keep a simple but delicious cake on top of my counter at all times, displayed under this spectacular dome. My kitchen has never looked prettier or more inviting, and the family sweet tooth has never been more satisfied. I've also noticed a marked increase in the number of friends "just happening to be passing by," none of whom turn down a piece of the day's cake.

I used to keep a cookie jar stocked for these purposes, but the idea of always having a cake on display in my pretty cake keeper inspired me to change my routine. It also inspired this book, a collection of old-fashioned recipes, many with a modern twist, for cakes you can bake quickly and easily. As I worked my way through recipes for Citrus and Black Pepper Pound Cake, Neoclassic Gingerbread, and Dulce de Leche Coffee Cake, I realized that it was often quicker and easier to bake a cake than to bake a batch of cookies. These unfrosted, unfilled cakes had short ingredient lists and could often be mixed in just one bowl. Unlike cookies, which are baked in many carefully watched batches, a simple cake requires little attention once it is popped into the oven. I thought back to the good old days, before cake was relegated to special occasions, when recipes for plain cake were in every home baker's repertoire. Offering updated versions of old favorites (Peach-Buttermilk Upside-Down Cake, Blueberry Buckle) and innovative recipes developed to excite today's sophisticated but busy bakers (Apricot and Olive Oil Cake, Pistachio-Polenta Pound Cake), a collection of this kind would restore cake to its rightful place as too simple and delicious to reserve for birthdays and anniversaries.

After baking and eating cake every day for almost a year, I'm excited to share the results in *Cake Keeper Cakes*, a collection of 100 recipes for unadorned cakes, moist and luscious, but simple to make and keep on hand for everyday eating. I've tried hard to develop recipes in line with the way people cook today. Like many home cooks, I like to make everyday dinners interesting by including foods and flavors from around the world.

I've included cakes I made to end a meal of pasta (Espresso-Hazelnut Bundt Cake), to match Thai chicken with basil (Pineapple and Toasted Coconut Cake), and to follow Moroccan lamb kebabs (Honey and Walnut Cake). Although the recipes in this book were designed to be simple enough to bake in the space between homework and dinnertime, many are interesting enough to present with a flourish at the end of a dinner party. Throughout,

I offer suggestions for transforming plain cakes into impressive desserts. There is a quick recipe for blueberries in basil syrup that is wonderful with Sour Cream and Lemon Cake. Slices of homey Apple and Cheddar Cheese Cake can be garnished with dollops of maple-flavored whipped cream. Slices of Anise Pound Cake can be served with a dried fruit and brandy compote and small scoops of vanilla ice cream.

The Cake Pans

WHEN I FIRST BEGAN this book, I found myself turning to the same six pans I already had in my kitchen: an 8-inch square pan, a 9-inch round pan, a 9-inch loaf pan, a 12-cup Bundt® pan, a springform pan, and an angel food cake pan. If you are in the market for a new pan, here are some shopping tips to help you buy one that will serve you best.

8-inch Square Pan: Nonstick is nice, but any aluminum baking pan, well greased, will do for these recipes. Don't be tempted to use a Pyrex® or ceramic baking dish, which is not as effective for browning cakes and baking them through evenly.

9-inch Round Pan: When I started to bake upside-down cakes for this book, I got nervous about fruit and caramel sticking to the bottom of my aluminum pan. So I went out and bought a Williams-Sonoma Goldtouch™ nonstick round cake pan with 2-inch sides. Every upside-down cake I baked in it released effortlessly. Nonstick baking pans with dark surfaces tend to overbrown cakes. Not this one—the golden surface browned them to perfection.

9-inch Loaf Pan: Again, nonstick is not essential, since running a paring knife around the edges of a well-greased pan is enough to release a cake cleanly. I use an old Baker's Secret® pan that I bought when I made my first banana bread, and it still works fine.

12-cup Bundt Pan: After upside-down cakes, Bundt cakes are the most likely to stick to a pan. If you need a new one, definitely buy a Bundt pan with a nonstick surface. Avoid intricate novelty shapes with nooks and crannies that love to trap cake batter.

Springform Pan: A springform pan with spring-release sides is essential for making cakes that shouldn't be inverted. These include crumb cakes, which would lose all their crumbs if turned upside down. Look for a pan without a lip around the bottom edge, which can get in the way of releasing and slicing the cake.

Angel Food Cake Pan: This is a large tube pan with a removable bottom and "feet" that allow air to circulate underneath the inverted cake as it cools in the pan on the countertop. For high-rising angel food and chiffon cakes, don't use a pan with a nonstick surface. They should be able to cling to the insides of the pan as they cool, maintaining their shape rather than shrinking and deflating.

Other Cake-Baking Equipment

ASIDE FROM the six essential pans listed previously, you will need the following items to bake cakes with ease:

Cake Testers: You can use a wooden toothpick to test doneness. I also like thin bamboo skewers.

Electric Mixer: Cakes made with vegetable oil or melted butter can be mixed by hand, but cakes requiring creaming and cakes requiring whipped egg whites are much easier to make with an electric mixer. But a good-quality hand mixer (look for one with thin wire beaters rather than old-fashioned beaters with metal shafts going down the center) will cream butter and sugar and whip egg whites very well, although a bit more slowly.

Fine Strainer: Good for sifting cocoa powder and confectioners' sugar.

continued

How to Swap Cake Pans in a Recipe

YOU LIKE THE IDEA of an Apple and Cheddar Cheese Cake, but instead of baking it in a round pan and slicing it into wedges, you'd like to bake it in a square pan and cut it into squares. Will it work? Absolutely, since a 9-inch round pan and an 8-inch square pan both have the same volume, 6 cups.

But substituting one pan for another isn't always so simple. A 9-inch loaf pan also has an equivalent volume. Doubling the recipe, you could fill a 12-cup Bundt pan. But baking a relatively heavy batter like apple and cheddar cheese in a narrow, deep pan may not work as well as baking it in a shallow one. The batter will have difficulty rising to an adequate height, and the edges of the cake may dry out before the interior is baked through.

For best results, substitute pans with caution, paying attention to volume and being sensitive to the type of batter you are working with. Some simple math and a little common sense should help you decide whether or not to risk a substitution.

Measuring Cups and Spoons: Precise measuring is essential for proper baking. Use clear "liquid" measuring cups for liquid ingredients. Liquid measuring cups with spouts are also handy for slowly adding liquid ingredients to a mixing bowl. Use plastic or metal "dry" measuring cups for large quantities of dry ingredients, and use measuring spoons for small quantities. Fill cups and spoons completely and level off with a knife for precise measurements.

Mixing Bowls: Large bowls will hold cake batter; smaller bowls are good for organizing ingredients before you start to bake. Buy sets of easy-to-store stainless steel and glass nesting bowls, and you will be set.

Parchment Paper: Line cake pans with circles of parchment, and you will never have to worry about sticking.

Spatulas: Rubber spatulas are necessary for scraping down the sides of a mixing bowl and smoothing batters once they are in the pan.

Wire Racks: You should have at least two wire racks for cooling cakes. Invert your cake pan onto one rack, and then re-invert the released cake onto the other to cool it completely.

Wire Whisk: Combine dry ingredients thoroughly with a wire whisk before adding to cake batter.

Ingredients

THE CAKES IN THE BOOK are simple to make. But to be spontaneous, you need to have your ingredients on hand. Here are the items I stock in my pantry, refrigerator, and freezer so I can bake at a moment's notice.

Baking Powder and Baking Soda: These chemical leaveners are responsible for the nice rise and light crumb of many of these cakes. They'll keep for months in the pantry.

Butter: All the recipes in this book call for unsalted butter. It has a purer flavor than salted butter and is more suitable for cake.

Buttermilk: Buttermilk gives many home-style cakes a slightly tangy flavor and wonderfully moist crumb. In addition, it helps cakes rise to incredible heights. Buttermilk will keep in the refrigerator for three weeks.

Chocolate: I keep several types of chocolate in my pantry for cake baking. In general, the chocolate cakes in this book are made with unsweetened cocoa powder. I like Dutch process cocoa powder for its rich chocolate taste and dark color. Occasionally, I'll add some unsweetened chocolate to a cake batter made with cocoa powder to give it an even deeper chocolate flavor. I could really use a bottomless bag of semisweet chocolate chips because they are great for adding flavor to a pumpkin or banana cake.

Cornmeal: Cornmeal adds flavor, color, and crunch to so many of my cakes. I think yellow is tastier than white, and I prefer stone-ground cornmeal for its superior flavor and nutritional value.

Dried Fruit: Raisins, apricots, prunes, and figs all add fruit flavor to a cake without making it soggy. Look for plump dried fruit and store it in an airtight container so it doesn't lose moisture over time.

Eggs: Eggs are packaged according to weight. All of these recipes call for large eggs, which weigh 2 ounces, for the sake of precision.

Flour: I rarely use cake flour to make the cakes in this book, since I want them to be pleasantly sturdy rather than meltingly tender (the exception is pound cake). I prefer unbleached all-purpose flour, which has more protein and provides more structure than cake flour. I avoid bleached flour because of the slight but discernible aftertaste. I use the King Arthur® brand, which is available in supermarkets and online, but other high-quality unbleached brands include Heckers®, Pillsbury®, and Gold Medal®.

Nuts: Nuts add richness, texture, and flavor to cakes. They spoil quickly, so keep them fresh by storing them in zipper-lock bags in the freezer.

continued

Salt: Table salt is inexpensive and does the trick in these recipes. Every once in a while, I'll use expensive sea salt (as in Pear Cake with Sea Salt Caramel) when it really makes a difference.

Sour Cream: Like buttermilk, sour cream adds flavor and moisture to cakes. Use only full-fat sour cream; reduced-fat and nonfat sour cream won't deliver the same taste and texture.

Sugar: Granulated, light brown, and dark brown sugar all have their place in this book. Store them in airtight containers or zipper-lock bags in the pantry. Keep confectioners' sugar on hand to sift over cakes just before serving.

Vanilla Extract: Pure vanilla extract brings a far superior flavor and aroma to baked goods than artificial extract.

Vegetable Oil: I use canola oil in cake recipes calling for vegetable oil, but any flavorless vegetable oil will work.

Vegetable Shortening: I use vegetable shortening for greasing pans. Buy it in small tubs, since it spoils quickly.

Toasting Nuts

IT'S NOT ABSOLUTELY NECESSARY to toast nuts before chopping them and stirring them into cake batter, but if you have the time to take this extra step, you will be bringing out the most of their delicious flavor. Another bonus: As nuts toast, they dry out and are less likely to become unpleasantly oily when finely ground in a food processor. Spread nuts in an even layer on a baking sheet and toast them in a 350°F oven until they are fragrant and just starting to color, 5 to 8 minutes. Watch them carefully. Very shortly after they color, they will burn to a crisp! Transfer the hot nuts to a plate and let them cool completely before chopping them as directed in the recipe.

Greasing Your Pans

IT IS A SAD, SAD THING when the cake you've baked and are eagerly anticipating eating refuses to come out of the pan or, even worse, mostly comes out of the pan, except for a $1/2$-inch layer that remains stuck to the bottom. To avoid this tragedy, follow the recipe's instructions for preparing the pan.

Some cakes require just a thin layer of grease. Some need to be greased and floured (or dusted with cocoa powder in the case of chocolate cakes). Occasionally, with sticky cakes baked in round pans, it is necessary to grease and flour the pan, lay a circle of parchment paper over the bottom, and grease and flour the parchment. Follow greasing and flouring instructions, even if you are using nonstick bakeware.

I prefer solid vegetable shortening over butter or nonstick cooking spray when baking these cakes. Although the idea of using butter for its superior flavor is appealing, the reality is that butter can cause overbrowning of the crust and is less reliable than shortening when it comes to making the inside of a pan slippery. Flavor is a nonissue, since most of these cake batters contain so much butter that an extra few teaspoons greasing the pan won't have a discernible impact on taste anyway. As for nonstick cooking spray, it tends to bead up on the surface of a pan, each bead absorbing flour or cocoa powder from dusting. The result is an unappetizing speckling of greasy flour globules covering the surface of the baked cake. Vegetable shortening, in contrast, even when topped with a coating of flour, melts invisibly into the cake as it bakes, leaving behind no such layer. This is an important consideration, since in most cases the cakes in this book will not be covered with frosting and need to be attractive straight out of the pan. If you see Baker's Joy®, a combination of vegetable oil and flour in a spray form, at your supermarket, snap up a few cans. It works just as well as vegetable shortening and flour, but in one step and with less mess.

To grease a pan, use a stiff pastry brush to cover the bottom and sides with a thin layer of vegetable shortening. Alternatively, scoop a teaspoon or two of shortening onto a paper towel and rub the shortening onto the bottom and sides of the pan, being sure to get into all the nooks and crannies if the pan happens to be a fancy Bundt mold. To dust a pan with flour or cocoa powder, sprinkle a tablespoonful into the pan, hold it at a slight angle, and tap the bottom edge gently on the counter as you rotate it, coating the bottom and the sides. Tap any excess flour into the sink when you are done. If necessary, trace and cut a circle of parchment the same size as the pan bottom, place it in the bottom of the greased and floured pan, and grease and flour the parchment using the same technique.

Mixing Techniques

THE RECIPES IN THIS BOOK are straightforward and uncomplicated. Most of them follow a similar format: Cream together butter and sugar, add wet and dry ingredients, pour the batter into the pan, and bake. But a lot of complex chemical reactions must occur during this seemingly simple process in order to achieve the goal: a tender, light, moist cake. Attention to the following details will help you get there:

Soften butter before creaming: The lightness of many cakes depends on incorporating an adequate amount of air into butter during creaming. This air, in the heat of the oven, will expand, causing the cake to rise. Cold butter won't hold as much air as room-temperature butter, so if you don't allow your butter to soften adequately, your cake won't rise to its fullest potential. At the same time, it is important not to let it get too soft. If butter gets too soft during creaming, the milk solids will separate from the fat, causing the whipped butter to deflate and become

oily. To determine that your butter is of the right consistency, press on it with a fingertip. You should be able to make a slight indentation, but the butter should still feel cool to the touch and not look too shiny or feel too slippery.

Cream butter and sugar adequately: When sugar and softened butter are creamed together, the sugar crystals act like little whisks, whipping air into the butter with their spinning action. This can take several minutes. At first, the mixture will look lumpy and rough. Then, it will become smooth, flattened against the sides of the bowl by the mixer's paddle attachment. Eventually, the butter and sugar mixture will become fluffy and lightened in color, signs for you to proceed to the next step.

Bring liquid ingredients to room temperature: Eggs, milk, buttermilk, and sour cream should also be at room temperature before they are added to a cake batter. At room temperature, they will combine with the butter and sugar into a smooth emulsion. Too cold, and they will cause the batter to be lumpy and heavy and prevent the cake from rising adequately.

Don't just dump: Add ingredients slowly, so they can be absorbed into the larger mixture.

Use your spatula: Scrape down the sides of your bowl at every stage of mixing, to make sure that there won't be clumps of ingredients that will spoil your cake's even crumb when it is baked.

A Few Oven Tips

PREHEAT YOUR OVEN as directed and, unless a recipe specifies otherwise, center your cake on the middle oven rack, where the heat is most even.

Occasionally, a recipe will instruct you to keep an eye on your cake as it nears completion, tenting it with foil if it looks like it may burn before it is baked through. I've noted particular recipes (usually ones with a lot of sugar or with another sweetener, such as honey, that tends to burn) where I found this step necessary, but it is a good idea to keep an eye on every cake with this in mind, since your oven may bake differently from mine.

How to Tell if Your Cake Is Done

BAKE YOUR CAKE for the minimum amount of time suggested in the recipe before opening the oven to check on its progress. Checking earlier will not only cool down the oven; it may, in the case of delicate batters, cause a dismaying collapse.

Once this danger has passed, take a look at the cake. Is the surface dry, not moist? Are the edges just beginning to pull away from the pan? When you lightly press a finger into the cake, does it spring back? If so, then it is probably done. To be certain, insert a toothpick into the center. If it comes out dry, then remove the cake. If not, let the cake bake another few minutes and check again.

Cooling Your Cake

THE INTOXICATING AROMA of a freshly baked cake can try your patience. But you must wait to let it cool properly in order to cut it into neat slices. From the oven, transfer your cake, still in its pan, to a wire rack and let it stand for 5 to 15 minutes (angel food cakes and chiffon cakes have their own cooling regime, which is discussed on page 149). To remove the cake from the pan, place a wire rack on top of it and, wearing oven mitts, invert the cake onto the rack. Re-invert it onto a second rack and let it cool completely before sliding it onto a serving platter or cake stand. Use a sharp serrated knife to cut clean slices or squares.

Do wait at least 30 minutes for round cakes (1 hour for thicker loaf and Bundt cakes), but be forewarned that slicing at this point may cause crumbling.

Storing Your Cake

TO MAKE SURE that your leftovers taste as great as your freshly baked cake, store them under a cake dome, in a cake keeper, or wrapped in a double layer of plastic wrap. If you have cut into your cake, the exposed surface of the interior will dry out slightly. Either cut away the dry portion of cake before cutting new slices, or press a piece of plastic wrap against the cut edge to prevent it from drying out.

Super-Delicious Whole-Wheat Carrot Cake—recipe on page 27

For some reason, cakes baked in my trusty 8-inch square baking pan seem less intimidating and more casual than any other shape of cake in my repertoire. Maybe it's the pan itself, which reminds me of the pan I baked brownies in when I was a kid, before I ever dared to bake a cake of any kind. How could anything baked in a brownie pan be difficult to make?

None of the cakes in this chapter are even remotely fancy, since they're designed for the most casual occasions: coffee breaks, after-school and bedtime snacks, breakfast the next day (don't worry, no one's judging you!). But that doesn't mean they aren't special. In fact, the simple form can inspire some really appealing flavor combinations: chocolate cake with stout, gingerbread with blueberries and maple syrup, strawberries and white chocolate, spice cake with orange zest and cranberries.

If there is anything tricky about baking these cakes, it is judging their doneness. As with brownies, the edges of the cake will bake through more quickly than the center, and they will dry out if overbaked. But if you pull the cake out of the oven before the center is set, the cake will sink in the middle. Watch it carefully and pull it from the oven just as soon as the edges start to pull away from the sides of the pan and a cake tester inserted into the center of the cake comes out clean, so the edges and the center are both properly baked.

Most of these cakes will release easily from the pan with a light greasing, but I recommend flouring the pan anyway, just in case the bottom of your cake is still a little moist and sticky when it comes out of the oven. If you don't intend to cut a snacking cake into nine squares right away, you can let the cake cool completely in the pan and cut and serve squares directly from the pan as needed, keeping uneaten cake fresh by covering the pan tightly with plastic wrap.

1½ cups unbleached all-purpose flour

1 teaspoon baking powder

1 teaspoon ground cinnamon

¼ teaspoon ground cloves

¼ teaspoon baking soda

¼ teaspoon salt

1 cup packed light brown sugar

6 tablespoons (¾ stick) unsalted butter, softened

1 cup apricot jam

2 eggs, room temperature

3 tablespoons sour cream

½ cup toasted and skinned hazelnuts, cooled and finely chopped

Apricot Jam Cake

HERE IS AN OLD-FASHIONED jam and spice cake recipe, made incredibly fragrant with the addition of toasted and chopped hazelnuts. Apricot jam is my favorite, but you can use strawberry, raspberry, or any other favorite jam with good results. The cake has an open, soft crumb and a wonderfully sweet and crunchy crust. If you'd like to garnish it, spoonfuls of tart sour cream or crème fraîche would nicely offset its sweetness. The batter is heavy from all of the jam, and it won't support a very high rise, so take care not to overmix it, beating in too much air, or the bubbles will burst in the oven, causing your cake to sink in the middle.

1. Preheat the oven to 350°F. Grease an 8-inch square baking pan and dust it with flour, knocking out any extra.

2. Whisk together the flour, baking powder, cinnamon, cloves, baking soda, and salt in a medium bowl.

3. Combine the butter and sugar in a large mixing bowl and cream with an electric mixer on medium-high speed until fluffy, about 3 minutes, scraping down the sides of the bowl once or twice as necessary. Beat in the jam until smooth.

4. With the mixer on medium-low speed, add the eggs one at a time. Add the sour cream. Scrape down the sides of the bowl. With the mixer on low speed, add the flour mixture a little at a time, scraping down the sides of the bowl after each addition and beating just until incorporated. Stir in the nuts on low speed.

5. Pour the batter into the prepared pan. Bake until a toothpick inserted in the center comes out clean, 50 minutes to 1 hour. Let the cake cool in the pan for 15 minutes, invert it onto a wire rack, and then turn it right side up again to cool completely. Cut into 9 squares and serve.

6. Store uneaten squares in a cake keeper or wrap in plastic and store at room temperature for up to 3 days.

Blackberry-Pecan Snack Cake

THE BERRIES AND PECAN topping melt together into a dark and delicious jam-like topping. Frozen berries are fine here, and you can use raspberries or blueberries instead of blackberries if you'd like.

MAKE THE STREUSEL

1. Preheat the oven to 350°F. Grease an 8-inch square baking pan and dust it with flour, knocking out any extra.

2. Combine the brown sugar, flour, cinnamon, and pecans in a mixing bowl. Work the butter pieces into the mixture, making coarse crumbs.

MAKE THE CAKE

1. Whisk together the sour cream, egg, and vanilla in a large measuring cup.

2. Combine the flour, baking powder, baking soda, salt, cloves, and nutmeg in a medium mixing bowl.

3. Combine the butter and sugar in a large mixing bowl and cream with an electric mixer on medium-high speed until fluffy, about 3 minutes, scraping down the sides of the bowl once or twice as necessary. With the mixer on low, slowly add the egg mixture and mix until well combined, scraping down the sides of the bowl once or twice as necessary. Add the flour mixture, 1/2 cup at a time, scraping down the sides of the bowl after each addition.

4. Scrape the batter into the prepared pan and smooth the top with a rubber spatula. Scatter the berries over the batter. Scatter the streusel over the berries. Bake the cake until it is golden and a toothpick inserted in the center comes out clean, about 45 minutes. Let the cake cool in the pan for 15 minutes, invert it onto a wire rack, and then turn it right side up again to cool completely. Cut into 9 squares and serve.

5. Store uneaten squares in a cake keeper or wrap in plastic and store at room temperature for up to 3 days.

Serves 9

FOR THE STREUSEL

6 tablespoons light brown sugar

1/4 cup unbleached all-purpose flour

1/2 teaspoon ground cinnamon

1/4 cup coarsely chopped pecans

2 tablespoons unsalted butter, cut into small pieces

FOR THE CAKE

1/2 cup sour cream

1 large egg

1 teaspoon pure vanilla extract

1 cup unbleached all-purpose flour

1/2 teaspoon baking powder

1/2 teaspoon baking soda

1/4 teaspoon salt

1/4 teaspoon ground cloves

1/4 teaspoon ground nutmeg

4 tablespoons (1/2 stick) unsalted butter, softened

1/2 cup sugar

1 cup fresh or frozen blackberries

13/4 cups unbleached all-purpose flour

3/4 cup unsweetened Dutch process cocoa powder

1 cup packed light brown sugar

1 teaspoon baking soda

1/2 teaspoon chipotle chili powder

1/4 teaspoon ground cinnamon

1/4 teaspoon salt

1 cup buttermilk

1/2 cup (1 stick) unsalted butter, melted

2 teaspoons pure vanilla extract

Chipotle-Chocolate Cake

A CLASSIC ONE-BOWL chocolate-buttermilk cake is a great vehicle for the Mexican flavors of chipotle chili powder and ground cinnamon. (Cayenne pepper will give a similar, but less smoky, kick if you don't have chipotle pepper on hand.) To make the squares dessert-worthy, serve each one with a cooling dollop of sweetened sour cream: Stir together 1 cup of sour cream with 2 tablespoons of dark brown sugar, 1/4 teaspoon of ground cinnamon, and 1/2 teaspoon of vanilla.

1. Preheat the oven to 350°F. Grease an 8-inch square baking pan and dust it with flour, knocking out any extra.

2. Combine the flour, cocoa powder, sugar, baking soda, chili powder, cinnamon, and salt in a large mixing bowl. With a wooden spoon or electric mixer, stir in the buttermilk, melted butter, and vanilla until just combined. It's okay if there are still a few lumps in the batter.

3. Scrape the batter into the prepared pan and smooth the top with a rubber spatula. Bake until a toothpick inserted in the center comes out clean, about 35 minutes. Let the cake cool in the pan for about 10 minutes, invert it onto a wire rack, and then turn it right side up on a rack to cool completely. Dust with cocoa powder and cut into 9 squares.

4. Store uneaten squares in a cake keeper or wrap in plastic and store at room temperature for up to 3 days.

Playing around with Chocolate Buttermilk Cake

ADDING CHILI POWDER to chocolate buttermilk cake is just one way to vary the very versatile recipe for basic chocolate buttermilk squares. You can use the recipe on page 16, minus the chili powder and cinnamon, to create a chocolate buttermilk cake tailored to your own tastes. Here are a few ideas to get you started:

*   Whisk 1/2 teaspoon of ground ginger into the flour mixture and 1/4 cup of finely chopped crystallized ginger into the batter for a ginger and chocolate combination.

*   Whisk 2 teaspoons of instant espresso powder into the flour mixture for a mocha buttermilk cake.

*   Stir 1 cup of peanut butter chips into the batter for a peanut butter cup effect. Use white chocolate chips for a black-and-white effect.

*   For German chocolate buttermilk cake, stir 1/2 cup of sweetened flaked coconut and 1/2 cup of finely chopped pecans into the batter.

Chocolate Cherry Snacking Cake

Serves 9

3 ounces unsweetened chocolate

1 large egg

1/2 cup buttermilk

1 teaspoon pure vanilla extract

1 cup unbleached all-purpose flour

1/4 teaspoon baking soda

1/4 teaspoon salt

1/2 cup (1 stick) unsalted butter, softened

1 cup sugar

1 cup dried cherries

A BROWNIE-LIKE CAKE made with unsweetened chocolate is the perfect medium for tart dried cherries. To make a brownie sundae–type dessert, you could serve these squares à la mode with whipped cream on top.

1. Preheat the oven to 350°F. Grease an 8-inch square baking pan and dust it with flour, knocking out any extra.

2. Put 1 inch of water in the bottom of a double boiler or a small saucepan and bring to a bare simmer. Place the chocolate in the top of the double boiler or in a stainless steel bowl big enough to rest on top of the saucepan, and set the bowl on top of the simmering water, making sure that the water doesn't touch the bottom of the bowl. Heat, whisking occasionally, until the chocolate is completely melted, 5 to 7 minutes. Set aside to cool.

3. Combine the egg, buttermilk, and vanilla in a glass measuring cup and lightly beat. Combine the flour, baking soda, and salt in a medium mixing bowl.

4. Combine the butter and sugar in a large mixing bowl and cream with an electric mixer on medium-high speed until fluffy, about 3 minutes, scraping down the sides of the bowl once or twice as necessary.

5. With the mixer on low, add 1/3 of the flour mixture and then 1/2 of the buttermilk mixture, scraping down the sides of the bowl after each addition. Repeat, ending with the remaining flour mixture. Stir in the cherries.

6. Scrape the batter into the prepared pan and smooth the top with a spatula. Bake until the cake is firm to the touch and a toothpick inserted in the center comes out clean, 35 to 40 minutes. Let the cake cool in the pan for 10 minutes, invert it onto a wire rack, and then turn it right side up on a rack to cool completely. Cut into 9 squares and serve.

7. Store uneaten squares in a cake keeper or wrap in plastic and store at room temperature for up to 3 days.

½ cup plus
3 tablespoons sugar

½ cup malted milk
powder

1 cup unbleached
all-purpose flour

6 tablespoons
unsweetened Dutch
process cocoa powder

¼ teaspoon salt

1½ teaspoons baking
powder

2 large eggs

¾ cup milk

6 tablespoons (¾ stick)
unsalted butter,
melted and cooled

1 teaspoon pure vanilla
extract

Chocolate Malted Snacking Cake

MALTED MILK POWDER somehow makes this chocolate snacking cake taste wholesome rather than decadent. It's a great after-school snack cake when served with a tall glass of milk. If this is too plain for your children's taste, you can cover the top of the cake with a half recipe of the chocolate ganache glaze on page 130 (without the chopped Butterfinger® bar) and sprinkle the glaze with ½ cup of crushed malted milk balls.

1. Preheat the oven to 350°F. Grease an 8-inch square baking pan and dust it with flour, knocking out any extra.

2. Combine the sugar, malted milk powder, flour, cocoa powder, salt, and baking powder in a large mixing bowl. With a wooden spoon or electric mixer, stir in the eggs, milk, butter, and vanilla until just combined.

3. Scrape the batter into the prepared pan and smooth the top with a rubber spatula. Bake until a toothpick inserted in the center comes out clean, 35 to 40 minutes. Let the cake cool in the pan for about 10 minutes. Invert it onto a wire rack, and then turn it right side up on a rack to cool completely.

4. Store uneaten squares in a cake keeper or wrap in plastic and store at room temperature for up to 3 days.

Chocolate Gingerbread

YOU CAN CAPITALIZE on chocolate's natural affinity for ginger by adding cocoa powder to gingerbread batter, along with a generous amount of mini chocolate chips. Vary the spices, too—a little black pepper and some instant espresso powder go well with the darker cake.

1. Preheat the oven to 350°F. Grease an 8-inch square baking pan and dust it with flour, knocking out any extra.

2. Stir together the hot water and molasses. Set aside to cool.

3. Sift together the flour, cocoa powder, baking soda, salt, ginger, espresso powder, cinnamon, cloves, and pepper in a medium mixing bowl.

4. Combine the butter and sugar in a large mixing bowl and cream with an electric mixer on medium-high speed until fluffy, about 3 minutes, scraping down the sides of the bowl once or twice as necessary.

5. Add the egg yolk and beat until smooth, scraping down the sides of the bowl once or twice as necessary. Beat in half the molasses mixture on low and then half the flour mixture. Scrape down the bowl and repeat with the remaining molasses mixture and the remaining flour mixture. Stir in the chocolate chips.

6. Scrape the batter into the prepared pan and smooth the top with a rubber spatula. Bake until a toothpick inserted in the center comes out clean, about 30 minutes. Let the gingerbread cool in the pan for about 15 minutes, invert it onto a wire rack, and then turn it right side up on a rack to cool completely. Cut into 9 squares and serve.

7. Store uneaten squares in a cake keeper or wrap in plastic and store at room temperature for up to 3 days.

Serves 9

¾ cup hot tap water

½ cup dark molasses

1 cup unbleached all-purpose flour

¼ cup unsweetened Dutch process cocoa powder

1 teaspoon baking soda

¼ teaspoon salt

1½ teaspoons ground ginger

½ teaspoon instant espresso powder

½ teaspoon ground cinnamon

¼ teaspoon ground cloves

¼ teaspoon ground black pepper

4 tablespoons (½ stick) unsalted butter, softened

½ cup firmly packed light brown sugar

1 large egg yolk

½ cup mini semisweet chocolate chips

FOR THE CARAMEL TOPPING

1 cup plus 2 tablespoons packed light brown sugar

¾ cup water

1 tablespoon unsalted butter

¼ teaspoon salt

FOR THE CAKE

2 cups unbleached all-purpose flour

2 teaspoons baking powder

2½ teaspoons ground cinnamon

½ teaspoon salt

2 tablespoons unsalted butter, softened

1 cup granulated sugar

1 cup whole milk

1 teaspoon pure vanilla extract

Cinnamon Pudding Cake

WHEN I FIRST TRIED THIS ONE, I had my doubts. I found myself pouring an ocean of brown sugar dissolved in water on top of the unbaked cake batter. The liquid sank to the bottom of the pan and thickened so that when the cake was overturned, it was bathed in gooey caramel sauce. This cake is irresistible warm from the oven, served with vanilla ice cream. As you can imagine, the topping gets very sticky, so use nonstick cooking spray on the pan and wait 15 minutes for the cake to firm up before serving.

MAKE THE TOPPING

1. Preheat the oven to 350°F. Spray the bottom and sides of an 8-inch square baking pan with nonstick cooking spray.

2. Combine the brown sugar, water, butter, and salt in a small saucepan and bring to a boil, whisking occasionally. Set aside to cool.

MAKE THE CAKE

1. Combine the flour, baking powder, cinnamon, and salt in a medium mixing bowl.

2. Combine the butter and granulated sugar in a large mixing bowl and cream with an electric mixer on medium-high speed until fluffy, about 2 minutes.

3. With the mixer on medium-low speed, add ⅓ of the flour mixture to the bowl. Add ½ of the milk and the vanilla. Add another ⅓ of the flour. Add the remaining milk and then the remaining flour. Scrape down the sides of the bowl and beat on medium speed for 30 seconds.

4. Scrape the batter into the prepared pan and smooth the top with a rubber spatula. Pour the topping over the batter (the pan will be very full). Carefully transfer the pan to the oven and bake until set, 45 to 50 minutes.

5. Let the cake cool in the pan for 15 minutes, invert it onto a large rimmed serving platter, and serve warm.

6. Let leftover squares cool completely and store in a cake keeper or airtight container at room temperature for up to 1 day or in the refrigerator for 3 days.

Fresh Strawberry Cake
with White Chocolate Chips

I TRIED A NUMBER of different, more complicated strawberry cakes before I came up with this one, my favorite. Made with juicy local berries (toss them with some flour before folding them into the batter, so your cake won't be pink), a little lemon zest, and chunks of white chocolate, this snacking cake is a pure and simple pleasure.

Serves 9

1 large egg

1 large egg yolk

$1/2$ cup sour cream

$1/2$ teaspoon grated lemon zest

2 teaspoons pure vanilla extract

$1 1/2$ cups unbleached all-purpose flour

$1 1/2$ teaspoons baking powder

$3/4$ teaspoon baking soda

$1/4$ teaspoon salt

6 tablespoons ($3/4$ stick) unsalted butter, softened

1 cup sugar

8 ounces strawberries, stemmed and sliced

1 cup white chocolate chips or chunks

1. Preheat the oven to 350°F. Grease an 8-inch square baking pan and dust it with flour, knocking out any extra. Combine the egg, egg yolk, sour cream, lemon zest, and vanilla in a large glass measuring cup and lightly beat. Combine $1 1/4$ cups flour, the baking powder, baking soda, and salt in a medium mixing bowl.

2. Combine the butter and sugar in a large mixing bowl and cream with an electric mixer on medium-high speed until fluffy, about 3 minutes, scraping down the sides of the bowl once or twice as necessary.

3. With the mixer on medium-low speed, pour the egg mixture into the bowl in a slow stream, stopping the mixer once or twice to scrape down the bowl.

4. Turn the mixer on low speed and add the flour mixture, $1/2$ cup at a time, scraping down the sides of the bowl after each addition. After the last addition, mix for 30 seconds on medium speed.

5. Combine the strawberries and remaining $1/4$ cup of flour in a medium bowl and toss to coat. Fold the flour-covered berries along with the chocolate chips into the batter with a rubber spatula.

6. Scrape the batter into the prepared pan and smooth the top with a spatula. Bake the cake until it is golden and a toothpick inserted in the center comes out clean, 45 to 50 minutes. Let the cake cool in the pan for about 5 minutes, invert it onto a wire rack, and then turn it right side up on a rack to cool completely. Cut into 9 squares and serve.

7. Store uneaten squares in a cake keeper or wrap in plastic and store at room temperature for up to 3 days.

FOR THE CAKE

8 whole graham crackers, finely ground (about 1 cup)

1/4 cup unbleached all-purpose flour

1 teaspoon baking powder

1/4 teaspoon salt

6 tablespoons (3/4 stick) unsalted butter, softened

1/4 cup sugar

1 large egg

1 large egg yolk

1 teaspoon pure vanilla extract

1/4 cup milk

1/2 cup semisweet chocolate chips

FOR THE FROSTING

1/2 cup (1 stick) unsalted butter, softened

1/2 cup confectioners' sugar

1/2 teaspoon pure vanilla extract

1/2 cup Marshmallow Fluff®

Graham Cracker– Chocolate Chip Snacking Cake

THIS CAKE WAS INSPIRED by the flavors of s'mores and is guaranteed to bring back memories of Girl Scout campfires. Grind your own crumbs for the freshest flavor.

MAKE THE CAKE

1. Preheat the oven to 350°F. Grease an 8-inch square baking pan and dust it with flour, knocking out any extra. Combine the graham cracker crumbs, flour, baking powder, and salt in a medium mixing bowl.

2. Combine the butter and sugar in a large mixing bowl and cream with an electric mixer on medium-high speed until fluffy, about 3 minutes, scraping down the sides of the bowl as necessary. With the mixer on low speed, add the egg, egg yolk, and vanilla. Scrape down the sides of the bowl and then beat until smooth.

3. With the mixer on low speed, add 1/3 of the flour mixture, then 1/2 of the milk, stirring until combined. Repeat with the remaining flour and milk, ending with the flour. Stir in the chocolate chips.

4. Scrape the batter into the prepared pan and smooth the top with a rubber spatula. Bake until a toothpick inserted in the center comes out clean, about 35 minutes. Let the cake cool in the pan for about 10 minutes. Invert it onto a wire rack, and then turn it right side up on a rack to cool completely.

MAKE THE FROSTING

1. Place the butter in a medium mixing bowl and beat until creamy. With the mixer on low speed, slowly add the sugar, scraping down the sides of the bowl as necessary. Stir in the vanilla and the Marshmallow Fluff and beat until smooth. Use immediately or cover the bowl with plastic wrap and keep it in the refrigerator for up to 3 days.

2. Cut the cake into squares and serve each one with a dollop of frosting on top (bring to room temperature first, if necessary). Store uneaten squares in a cake keeper or wrap in plastic and store at room temperature for up to 3 days.

½ cup pecans, toasted and finely chopped

1½ cups unbleached all-purpose flour

1 cup sugar

½ teaspoon baking soda

¼ teaspoon salt

½ teaspoon ground cinnamon

1 large egg

1 large egg yolk

6 tablespoons vegetable oil

½ cup sour cream

1 teaspoon pure vanilla extract

1 can crushed pineapple (8 ounces), drained

1 medium banana, mashed

Hummingbird Snacking Cake

HUMMINGBIRD CAKE, made with crushed pineapple and mashed banana, is usually baked in two layers and covered with a rich cream cheese frosting. But in my opinion, frosting such a rich and sweet cake would be gilding the lily. This cake is so chock full of flavors and textures that it is most enjoyable served in plain squares.

1. Preheat the oven to 350°F. Grease an 8-inch square baking pan and dust it with flour, knocking out any extra.

2. Combine the nuts, flour, sugar, baking soda, salt, and cinnamon in a large mixing bowl. With a wooden spoon or electric mixer, stir in the egg, egg yolk, oil, sour cream, and vanilla until just combined. It's okay if there are still a few lumps in the batter. Stir in the pineapple and banana.

3. Scrape the batter into the prepared pan and smooth the top with a rubber spatula. Bake until a toothpick inserted in the center comes out clean, about 35 minutes. Let the cake cool in the pan for about 10 minutes. Invert it onto a wire rack, and then turn it right side up on a rack to cool completely.

4. Store uneaten squares in a cake keeper or wrap in plastic and store at room temperature for up to 3 days.

Neoclassic Gingerbread

MOST GINGERBREAD IS MADE with ground ginger. Here I add some fresh ginger, to give this light and springy gingerbread some extra zing. Fresh ginger can be stringy and tough. I recommend grating it finely, rather than chopping it, so it melts into the batter during baking. For everyday eating, the squares need no embellishment.

1. Preheat the oven to 350°F. Grease an 8-inch square baking pan and dust it with flour, knocking out any extra.

2. Pour the hot water into a glass measuring cup and stir in the molasses and baking soda. Set aside to cool.

3. Combine the flour, baking powder, salt, ginger, cinnamon, and cloves in a medium mixing bowl.

4. Combine the butter and sugar in a large mixing bowl and cream with an electric mixer on medium-high speed until fluffy, about 3 minutes, scraping down the sides of the bowl once or twice as necessary. Stir in the fresh ginger.

5. Add the egg yolk and beat until smooth, scraping down the sides of the bowl once or twice as necessary. Beat in $1/2$ the molasses mixture on low speed and then $1/2$ the flour mixture. Scrape down the bowl and repeat with the remaining molasses mixture and the remaining flour mixture.

6. Scrape the batter into the prepared pan and smooth the top with a rubber spatula. Bake until a toothpick inserted in the center comes out clean, about 30 minutes. Let the gingerbread cool in the pan for about 15 minutes, invert it onto a wire rack, and then turn it right side up on a rack to cool completely. Cut into 9 squares and serve.

7. Store uneaten squares in a cake keeper or wrap in plastic and store at room temperature for up to 3 days.

Serves 9

- $3/4$ cup hot tap water
- $1/2$ cup dark molasses
- 1 teaspoon baking soda
- $1\frac{1}{4}$ cups unbleached all-purpose flour
- 1 teaspoon baking powder
- $1/4$ teaspoon salt
- 1 teaspoon ground ginger
- $1/2$ teaspoon ground cinnamon
- $1/4$ teaspoon ground cloves
- 4 tablespoons ($1/2$ stick) unsalted butter, softened
- $1/2$ cup firmly packed light brown sugar
- 1 tablespoon finely grated fresh ginger
- 1 large egg yolk

1 cup rolled oats
(not quick-cooking)

¾ cup boiling water

1½ cups unbleached
all-purpose flour

1½ teaspoons baking
powder

½ teaspoon cinnamon

¼ teaspoon salt

½ cup (1 stick) unsalted
butter, softened

1 cup packed light
brown sugar

½ cup granulated sugar

2 large eggs

1 teaspoon pure vanilla
extract

1 cup bittersweet or
semisweet chocolate
chips

1 cup finely chopped
walnuts or pecans

Oatmeal–Chocolate Chip Cake

THESE SQUARES TASTE like my favorite oatmeal–chocolate chip cookies but in cake form. If you prefer your oatmeal cookies with dates, you can use them here, too. Substitute 1 cup of finely chopped pitted dates for the chocolate chips, and add ⅛ teaspoon of ground nutmeg to the batter. Individually wrapped squares are great for lunch boxes, picnics, and long car rides.

1. Place the oats in a heatproof bowl. Pour the boiling water over the oatmeal. Let stand until cool.

2. Preheat the oven to 350°F. Grease an 8-inch square baking pan and dust it with flour, knocking out any extra.

3. Combine the flour, baking powder, cinnamon, and salt in a medium mixing bowl.

4. Combine the butter and sugars in a large mixing bowl and cream with an electric mixer on medium-high speed until fluffy, about 3 minutes, scraping down the sides of the bowl once or twice as necessary. Add the eggs and vanilla and beat until smooth. Stir in the oats.

5. With the mixer on low speed, add the flour mixture, ½ cup at a time, scraping down the sides of the bowl after each addition. Stir in the chocolate chips and nuts.

6. Scrape the batter into the prepared pan and smooth the top with a rubber spatula. Bake the cake until it is golden and a toothpick inserted in the center comes out clean, 50 to 55 minutes. Let the cake cool in the pan for about 10 minutes, invert it onto a wire rack, and then turn it right side up on a rack to cool completely. Cut into 9 squares and serve.

7. Store uneaten squares in a cake keeper or wrap in plastic and store at room temperature for up to 3 days.

Super-Delicious Whole-Wheat Carrot Cake

I NEVER LIKED CARROT CAKE because of its spongy, soggy texture. And the cream cheese and confectioners' sugar frosting slathered on top didn't help. So when devising my own carrot cake, I went for a less sticky and sweet version. Butter moistens the cake without making it greasy. It's melted, so the cake is just as easy to make as one-bowl versions made with oil. Some whole-wheat flour adds wholesome flavor. Instead of frosting, I serve this plain or with a dollop of sour cream sprinkled with brown sugar alongside each square.

Serves 9

1. Preheat the oven to 350°F. Coat the inside of an 8-inch square baking pan with cooking spray and dust with flour, knocking out any extra.

2. Whisk together the butter and brown sugar in a large mixing bowl. Whisk in the eggs and then the milk. Stir in the all-purpose flour, whole-wheat flour, baking powder, ground cinnamon, and salt until combined. Stir in the walnuts, raisins, and carrots.

3. Scrape the batter into the prepared pan and smooth the top with a rubber spatula. Bake the cake until it is golden and a toothpick inserted in the center comes out clean, 35 to 40 minutes. Let the cake cool in the pan for about 15 minutes, invert it onto a wire rack, and then turn it right side up on a rack to cool completely. Cut into 9 squares and serve.

4. Store uneaten squares in a cake keeper or wrap in plastic and store at room temperature for up to 3 days.

1/2 cup (1 stick) unsalted butter, melted and cooled

1 cup firmly packed light brown sugar

2 large eggs

1/4 cup milk

1 cup unbleached all-purpose flour

1/3 cup whole-wheat flour

1 teaspoon baking powder

1 teaspoon ground cinnamon

1/4 teaspoon salt

1/2 cup chopped walnuts

1/2 cup dark raisins

2 cups peeled and grated carrots (about 4 medium carrots)

FOR THE CAKE

1 large egg yolk

¼ cup pure maple syrup

½ cup buttermilk

1⅓ cups unbleached all-purpose flour

1 teaspoon baking soda

1 teaspoon ground ginger

½ teaspoon cinnamon

⅛ teaspoon ground cloves

¼ teaspoon salt

½ cup (1 stick) unsalted butter, softened

6 tablespoons sugar

1 cup dried blueberries

FOR THE ICING

2 tablespoons lemon juice

½ cup confectioners' sugar

Maple Syrup Gingerbread

HERE'S A LIGHTER STYLE of gingerbread, made with maple syrup and molasses, just great when you want something spicy but not too rich or heavy. The dried blueberries are a delicious match with the mild spices. The light lemon glaze adds a snap of acidity.

MAKE THE CAKE

1. Preheat the oven to 350°F. Grease an 8-inch square baking pan and dust it with flour, knocking out any extra.

2. Combine the egg yolk, maple syrup, and buttermilk in a large glass measuring cup and lightly beat. Combine the flour, baking soda, ginger, cinnamon, cloves, and salt in a medium mixing bowl.

3. Combine the butter and sugar in a large mixing bowl and cream with an electric mixer on medium-high speed until fluffy, about 3 minutes, scraping down the sides of the bowl once or twice as necessary.

4. With the mixer on medium-low speed, pour the buttermilk mixture into the bowl in a slow stream, stopping the mixer once or twice to scrape down the bowl.

5. Turn the mixer on low speed and add the flour mixture, ½ cup at a time, scraping down the sides of the bowl after each addition. After the last addition, mix for 30 seconds on medium speed. Stir in the blueberries.

6. Scrape the batter into the prepared pan and smooth the top with a spatula. Bake the cake until it is golden and a toothpick inserted in the center comes out clean, 35 to 40 minutes. Let the cake cool in the pan for about 5 minutes, invert it onto a wire rack, and then turn it right side up on a rack to cool completely.

MAKE THE ICING

1. Whisk together the lemon juice and confectioners' sugar. Pour the icing into the middle of the cooled cake and spread over the top with a small offset spatula, letting any excess drip over the sides. Let stand until the icing firms up, about 30 minutes. Cut into 9 squares and serve. Store uneaten squares in a cake keeper or wrap in plastic and store at room temperature for up to 3 days.

¾ cup poppy seeds

½ cup boiling water

1⅓ cups unbleached
all-purpose flour

2 teaspoons baking
powder

¼ teaspoon salt

14 tablespoons
(1¾ sticks) unsalted
butter, softened

1 cup sugar

4 large eggs

1 teaspoon pure vanilla
extract

1 teaspoon pure almond
extract

Confectioners' sugar
for dusting

Poppy Seed Cake

MOST POPPY SEED CAKES are crunchy from the seeds but don't have much of their wonderful flavor and aroma. To release real poppy seed flavor into your cake, don't skimp—I use ¾ cup of seeds in this 8-inch square cake—and soak and grind the seeds before adding them to the batter. Don't try grinding them before soaking—they're so hard that the blades of the blender will have no effect.

1. Place the poppy seeds in a heatproof bowl and cover with the boiling water. Cover the bowl with plastic wrap and let stand until the poppy seeds are softened, 1 to 3 hours. Transfer the seeds, which will have absorbed most of the water, to a blender and blend to slightly crush.

2. Preheat the oven to 350°F. Grease an 8-inch square baking pan and dust it with flour, knocking out any extra. Whisk together the flour, baking powder, and salt in a medium bowl.

3. Combine the butter and sugar in a large bowl and beat with an electric mixer until fluffy, about 3 minutes, scraping down the sides of the bowl as necessary. Add the poppy seed mixture and mix on medium speed, scraping down the sides of the bowl as necessary, until well combined.

4. Add the eggs, one at a time, scraping down the sides of the bowl after each addition. Stir in the vanilla and almond extracts.

5. Stir in the flour mixture until smooth.

6. Scrape the batter into the prepared pan and smooth the top with a rubber spatula. Bake until the cake is golden and a toothpick inserted in the center comes out clean, about 45 minutes. Let the cake cool in the pan for 10 minutes, invert it onto a wire rack, and cool completely. Dust heavily with powdered sugar, cut into 9 squares, and serve.

7. Store uneaten squares in a cake keeper or wrap in plastic and store at room temperature for up to 3 days.

1 cup sour cream, room temperature

4 large eggs, room temperature

1 teaspoon pure vanilla extract

2¼ cups cake flour

1 teaspoon baking powder

½ teaspoon baking soda

¼ teaspoon salt

4 tablespoons (½ stick) unsalted butter, softened

1¼ cups sugar

2 teaspoons finely grated lemon zest

¼ cup fresh lemon juice

Confectioners' sugar for dusting

Sour Cream and Lemon Cake

THIS COMBINATION MIGHT SOUND mouth-puckering, but the acidity in the sour cream and lemon cuts the buttery richness of this cake so the balance is just right. A dusting of confectioners' sugar is all it needs for a finish. To dress it up for a party, serve it with basil blueberries: Combine ½ cup water, ½ cup sugar, and 5 basil leaves in a small, heavy saucepan and bring to a boil. Remove from the heat and let stand 15 minutes. Strain and pour over 1 pint of blueberries.

1. Preheat the oven to 325°F. Grease an 8-inch square baking pan and dust it with flour, knocking out any extra.

2. Whisk together the sour cream, eggs, and vanilla in a large glass measuring cup. Whisk together the flour, baking powder, baking soda, and salt in a medium bowl.

3. Combine the butter and sugar in a large mixing bowl and cream with an electric mixer on medium-high speed until fluffy, about 3 minutes, scraping down the sides of the bowl once or twice as necessary.

4. With the mixer on medium-low speed, pour the sour cream mixture into the bowl in a slow stream, stopping the mixer once or twice to scrape down the bowl. Stir in the lemon zest and lemon juice. With the mixer on low speed, add the flour mixture a little at a time, scraping down the sides of the bowl after each addition and beating until smooth.

5. Pour the batter into the prepared pan. Bake until a toothpick inserted in the center comes out clean, about 40 minutes. Let the cake cool in the pan for 5 minutes, invert it onto a wire rack, and then turn it right side up again to cool completely. Dust with confectioners' sugar, cut into 9 squares, and serve.

6. Store uneaten squares in a cake keeper or wrap in plastic and store at room temperature for up to 2 days.

1½ cups cake flour

1 teaspoon baking powder

½ teaspoon baking soda

¼ teaspoon salt

¼ teaspoon ground cloves

½ cup sour cream

2 large eggs

¼ cup orange juice

1 teaspoon pure vanilla extract

½ cup (1 stick) unsalted butter, softened

¾ cup sugar

1 tablespoon grated orange zest

1 cup dried sweetened cranberries

Spiced Orange and Cranberry Snacking Cake

A DASH OF GROUND CLOVES gives this buttery orange and cranberry cake deep flavor. Try it with orange sorbet.

1. Preheat the oven to 350°F. Grease an 8-inch square baking pan and dust it with flour, knocking out any extra. Combine the flour, baking powder, baking soda, salt, and cloves in a medium mixing bowl. Combine the sour cream, eggs, orange juice, and vanilla in a large glass measuring cup and lightly beat.

2. Combine the butter and sugar in a large mixing bowl and cream with an electric mixer on medium-high speed until fluffy, about 3 minutes, scraping down the sides of the bowl once or twice as necessary. Stir in the orange zest.

3. With the mixer on medium-low speed, pour the egg mixture into the bowl in a slow stream, stopping the mixer once or twice to scrape down the sides.

4. Turn the mixer to low speed and add the flour mixture, ½ cup at a time, scraping down the sides of the bowl after each addition. After the last addition, mix for 30 seconds on medium speed. Stir in the cranberries.

5. Bake until the cake is golden and a toothpick inserted into the center comes out clean, 35 to 40 minutes. Let the cake cool in the pan for 15 minutes, invert it onto a wire rack, and then turn it right side up again to cool completely. Cut into 9 squares and serve.

6. Store uneaten squares in a cake keeper or wrap in plastic and store at room temperature for up to 3 days.

FOR THE CAKE

¹/₂ cup stout, such as Guinness®

¹/₂ cup (1 stick) unsalted butter, softened

6 tablespoons unsweetened Dutch process cocoa powder

1 cup unbleached all-purpose flour

1 cup packed light brown sugar

¹/₂ teaspoon baking soda

¹/₄ teaspoon salt

1 large egg, lightly beaten

¹/₃ cup sour cream

FOR THE CHOCOLATE-STOUT GLAZE

¹/₄ cup stout

2 tablespoons light corn syrup

4 ounces bittersweet chocolate, finely chopped

Stout and Chocolate Snacking Cake with Chocolate-Stout Glaze

BEER CONNOISSEURS will immediately recognize the distinctive flavor of stout in this luscious cake and frosting, but people not familiar with the dark brew will just wonder how you coaxed so much rich and interesting flavor from your cocoa powder. Don't skip the glaze. It is appealingly glossy, and its bittersweet snap adds a lot to the dessert.

MAKE THE CAKE

1. Preheat the oven to 350°F. Grease an 8-inch square baking pan and dust it with flour, knocking out any extra.

2. Combine the stout and butter in a saucepan and bring to a bare simmer. Remove from the heat and whisk in the cocoa powder until smooth. Set aside to cool.

3. Combine the flour, brown sugar, baking soda, and salt in a large mixing bowl. With a wooden spoon or electric mixer, stir in the stout mixture, egg, and sour cream until just combined. It's okay if there are still a few lumps in the batter.

4. Scrape the batter into the prepared pan and smooth the top with a rubber spatula. Bake until a toothpick inserted in the center comes out clean, about 35 minutes. Set the pan on a wire rack and let the cake cool completely in the pan.

MAKE THE GLAZE

1. Combine the stout and corn syrup in a small, heavy saucepan and bring to a boil. Remove from the heat and whisk in the chocolate until shiny and smooth. Let cool to warm room temperature and spread the sauce over the top of the cake. Let stand until the sauce is set, about 1 hour. Cut the cake into squares and serve.

2. Store uneaten squares in a cake keeper or wrap in plastic and store at room temperature for up to 3 days.

FOR THE SYRUP

3/4 cup sugar

6 tablespoons water

2 tablespoons lemon juice

Rind of 1 lemon, removed with a vegetable peeler in one piece

FOR THE CAKE

1 egg

3/4 cup quick-cooking Cream of Wheat®

3/4 cup sugar

7 tablespoons butter, melted and cooled

1 cup plain whole-milk yogurt or lowfat yogurt

2 tablespoons lemon juice

1/4 teaspoon baking soda

1/2 cup raisins

Semolina and Yogurt Cake

THIS GREEK SPECIALTY is something different, a syrup-soaked cake that is pudding-like in its moistness. But like many other cakes in this book, it is long-keeping and wonderful as a snack or for dessert, served with sweetened, softly whipped cream. When I saw it could be made with my all-time favorite hot cereal, Cream of Wheat, I had to try a version of my own.

MAKE THE SYRUP

1. Preheat the oven to 375°F. Grease an 8-inch square baking pan and dust it with flour, knocking out any extra.

2. Combine the sugar, water, lemon juice, and lemon rind in a small saucepan. Bring to a boil over high heat. Lower the heat and simmer for 10 minutes. Remove the pan from the heat and let cool to room temperature.

MAKE THE CAKE

1. Whisk together the egg, Cream of Wheat, sugar, and melted butter until smooth. Stir in the yogurt and lemon juice. Stir in the baking soda. Stir in the raisins.

2. Scrape the batter into the prepared pan and smooth the top with a rubber spatula. Bake the cake until it is golden and a toothpick inserted in the center comes out clean, 25 to 30 minutes.

3. Set the cake, still in the pan, on a wire rack. Slowly drizzle the cooled syrup all over the cake, letting it soak in. Cover tightly with plastic wrap and let stand until the syrup is absorbed, about 30 minutes. Unwrap and let the cake cool completely.

4. Slice into squares and serve.

5. Keep uneaten squares in the pan, covered in plastic wrap, for up to 1 day at room temperature and for up to 1 week in the refrigerator.

World's Quickest Yeasted Coffee Cake

Serves 9

3/4 cup whole milk

4 tablespoons (1/2 stick) unsalted butter

2 envelopes (1 1/2 tablespoons) instant yeast

1 3/4 cups unbleached all-purpose flour

1/2 teaspoon salt

1/4 cup granulated sugar

1 teaspoon ground cinnamon

1/3 cup dark corn syrup

3/4 cup packed light brown sugar

3/4 cup finely chopped pecans

I ADORE THIS RECIPE, adapted from one on the back of a Fleischmann's® yeast package. Not only is it wholesome and delicious, warm from the oven on a weekend morning, but it is amazingly, magically quick to make. Instead of letting the yeasted dough rise slowly on the countertop, you place the just-mixed dough in the pan with its topping, and then turn the oven on. The dough rises as the oven heats, and then bakes in just a few minutes more. This cake is best served warm from the oven, but you can reheat day-old squares in a 350°F oven for 5 minutes so they regain some of their just-baked goodness.

1. Grease an 8-inch square baking pan and dust it with flour, knocking out any extra.

2. Heat the milk and 2 tablespoons butter in a small saucepan until the butter is melted and the milk is very warm to the touch. Pour into a large mixing bowl and whisk in the yeast to dissolve. Stir in the flour and salt and beat with an electric mixer on medium-low speed until you have a sticky dough. Press the dough into the prepared pan.

3. Combine the granulated sugar and cinnamon in a small bowl. Sprinkle the cinnamon sugar evenly over the batter.

4. Melt the remaining 2 tablespoons of butter. Combine the corn syrup, brown sugar, and melted butter in a medium bowl and stir. Spread over the dough. Sprinkle pecans evenly across the top.

5. Place the pan in a cold oven. Turn the heat to 350°F. Bake until the cake is golden and set in the center, 25 to 30 minutes. Let cool slightly and serve warm.

CHAPTER 2

Round Cakes

Apple and Cheddar Cheese Cake—recipe on page 43

If I were stranded on a desert island that was equipped with an oven and a KitchenAid® mixer, but I was limited to only one cake pan, I'd choose my 9-inch round nonstick pan. This pan is so versatile that I could use it to mark time by counting the number of cakes I could bake in it. While waiting for my rescuers, I could whip up a Pear Cake with Sea Salt Caramel Sauce, a Honey and Walnut Cake, and an Apricot and Olive Oil Cake. When they finally arrived, I could gather some local mangoes for a celebration Mango Upside-Down Cake.

Imagining this scenario and other hardship situations calling for cake, I tried to come up with round cakes that were quick to make but not boring. The first half of the chapter consists of plain round cakes, most of them aiming to capture your interest with their intriguing ingredient combinations (Apple and Cheddar Cheese Cake) or interesting construction (Zebra Cake with striped vanilla and chocolate layers). Embellishments, where there are any, are ridiculously simple.

The second half of the chapter contains my upside-down cake recipes. These cakes take a bit more effort, but the payoff is a shiny fruit and caramel topping that serves as a stunning cake decoration. Unmolding an upside-down cake is a breeze if you use a high-quality nonstick cake pan (see page 4). But timing is important if you want your cake to look its best. If you invert the cake immediately, the topping will run down the sides of the cake instead of staying put. So let the cake cool in the pan for a few minutes to allow the topping to begin to set up before unmolding. But don't let the cake sit too long in the pan, or the caramel may bond with the metal. If a few pieces of fruit stick to the bottom of the pan, don't worry. You will easily see the impressions on top of the cake left by the fruit. Simply pick up the pieces and put them back where they belong.

10 tablespoons
  (1¼ sticks) unsalted
  butter

½ vanilla bean

1½ cups sliced almonds

1½ cups sugar

1 cup plus 2 tablespoons
  unbleached
  all-purpose flour

8 large egg whites

Pinch salt

2 tablespoons dark rum

Almond–Brown Butter Cake

THIS IS ADAPTED FROM a Nick Malgieri recipe, a classic financier cake that he generously shared with his cooking school students when I took his class. In my version, a vanilla bean steeped in browned butter lends the cake a wonderful aroma and nutty flavor.

1. Preheat the oven to 350°F. Grease a 9-inch round cake pan. Line the bottom of the pan with a circle of parchment paper. Grease the parchment. Dust the pan sides and parchment with flour.

2. Melt the butter in a small saucepan over medium-low heat. Split the vanilla bean and scrape the seeds into the butter. Add the scraped pod to the pan. Heat until the butter is light brown and gives off a nutty aroma, stirring frequently, about 5 minutes. Watch it carefully, because it will burn quickly after it browns. Remove from the heat and let stand for 10 minutes. Discard the vanilla bean and pour the butter through a fine strainer to remove the burnt solids. Set aside to cool.

3. Reserve ¼ cup of the almonds. Place the remaining 1¼ cups almonds and ¾ cup sugar in the bowl of a food processor and grind fine. Add the flour and pulse to combine.

4. Place the egg whites in a large mixing bowl with the salt and beat until foamy. With the mixer on high, add the remaining ¾ cup sugar in a slow, steady stream and whip until the whites are shiny and hold stiff peaks. Fold in the flour mixture in three additions, alternating with the butter mixture and ending with the flour. Fold in the rum.

5. Scrape the batter into the prepared pan and smooth with a spatula. Scatter the remaining ¼ cup of almonds over the batter. Bake until golden and a toothpick inserted into the center of the cake comes out dry, about 35 to 40 minutes.

6. Let the cake cool in the pan for 10 minutes, invert it onto a wire rack, and then turn it right side up again to cool completely. Dust heavily with powdered sugar before cutting into wedges, and serve.

7. Store uneaten cake in a cake keeper or wrap in plastic and store at room temperature for up to 2 days.

Apple *and* Cheddar Cheese Cake

GRATED CHEDDAR CHEESE melts into this cake and gives it a wonderfully tangy flavor and richness. Diced pear may be substituted for the apple if you like. Either way, it tastes great with maple syrup–sweetened whipped cream on the side.

1. Preheat the oven to 350°F. Grease a 9-inch round cake pan and dust with flour. Combine the flour, cornmeal, baking powder, and salt in a medium bowl.

2. Combine the butter and sugar in a large mixing bowl and cream with an electric mixer on medium-high speed until fluffy, about 3 minutes, scraping down the sides of the bowl once or twice as necessary. With the mixer on medium-low speed, add the eggs, one at a time, scraping down the sides of the bowl after each addition.

3. Turn the mixer to low speed and add $1/2$ of the flour mixture. Stir in the milk. Stir in the remaining flour mixture until just combined. Stir in the cheddar cheese and apple.

4. Scrape the batter into the prepared pan and smooth the top with a rubber spatula. Bake until the cake is golden brown and a toothpick inserted into the center comes out clean, about 35 minutes. Let the cake cool in the pan for about 10 minutes, invert it onto a wire rack, and then turn it right side up on a rack to cool completely.

5. Store uneaten cake in a cake keeper or wrap in plastic and store at room temperature for up to 2 days.

Serves 8

- $3/4$ cup unbleached all-purpose flour
- $1/2$ cup yellow cornmeal
- $1 1/2$ teaspoons baking powder
- $1/4$ teaspoon salt
- $1/2$ cup (1 stick) unsalted butter, softened
- $3/4$ cup sugar
- 2 eggs
- 6 tablespoons milk
- 1 cup grated cheddar cheese
- 1 large tart apple, such as a Granny Smith, peeled, cored, and cut into $1/4$-inch dice

2 cups unbleached all-purpose flour

1½ teaspoons baking powder

¼ teaspoon salt

1 cup sugar

⅔ cup extra-virgin olive oil

1 teaspoon lemon zest

3 large eggs

1 cup apricot nectar

1½ cups dried apricots, chopped

Apricot and Olive Oil Cake

EXTRA-VIRGIN OLIVE OIL lends moisture to this cake as well as its wonderful fragrance. The apricots add Mediterranean flavor (if they are not very plump and moist when you open the package, put them in a bowl and pour boiling water over them; soak for a minute and then pat them dry before proceeding). If you'd like, you can also throw in a handful of chopped unsalted pistachio nuts. Or even better—serve with small scoops of pistachio ice cream.

1. Preheat the oven to 375°F. Grease a 12-cup Bundt pan and dust it with flour, knocking out any extra. Whisk together the flour, baking powder, salt, and sugar in a large mixing bowl. Whisk together the olive oil, lemon zest, eggs, and apricot nectar in a medium mixing bowl.

2. Pour the olive oil mixture into the flour mixture and stir to combine.

3. Scrape about ⅔ of the batter into the prepared pan and scatter the apricots over the batter. Cover with the remaining batter and smooth with a spatula. Bake until a toothpick inserted into the center comes out clean, about 45 minutes. Let the cake cool in the pan for about 10 minutes and invert it onto a wire rack to cool completely. Slice and serve.

4. Store uneaten cake in a cake keeper or wrap in plastic and store at room temperature for up to 3 days.

Dressing Up a Plain Round Cake

ROUND CAKES, unfrosted and undecorated, appeal to the minimalist in me. The simplicity of a wedge of round cake served with a tall, cold glass of milk or a cup of tea never fails to please. But if you're serving this cake to friends at a dinner party, such a presentation might be too austere. Here are a few things to do with a plain round cake to step it up a notch:

Edible, Pesticide-Free Flowers

Daisies, violets, geraniums, and roses are all edible and may be used to garnish your cake plate and platter. Make sure your flowers are pesticide free by picking them from your own pesticide-free garden or checking with your florist. Stay away from flowers that are poisonous! These include daffodils, lily of the valley, and hydrangea. For full lists of edible and poisonous flowers, go to http://homecooking .about.com/od/specificfoo1/ a/flowertips.htm.

Whipped Cream Rosettes

Pipe whipped cream through a large (at least ¼-inch) pastry tip to create a rosette border at the edge of your cake. Let the rosettes be your guide as you slice.

Confectioners' Sugar or Cocoa Powder Stencil

Laying a round paper doily over the top of your cake, then sifting confectioners' sugar (or cocoa powder for chocolate cakes) over it before lifting away the doily creates a pretty lace pattern in seconds. Other easy stenciling ideas: cut-out letters, stars, and polka dots.

Candles

Customize your cake with attractive and fun candles. Sparklers are always festive. I also like the letter candles, each one attached to a wooden skewer, that spell out "Happy Birthday" or a guest of honor's name. Recently, I've seen cake candles in the shape of ruby slippers, rubber ducks, and bowling balls.

3 tablespoons unsweetened Dutch process cocoa powder plus more for dusting

3/4 cup unbleached all-purpose flour

1/2 teaspoon baking powder

1/4 teaspoon salt

1/2 teaspoon ground cinnamon

1/4 teaspoon ground coriander

1/4 teaspoon ground cloves

1/4 teaspoon ground nutmeg

1/2 cup (1 stick) unsalted butter, cut into small pieces

2 large eggs

2/3 cup sugar

1/4 cup hot tap water

1/2 cup finely chopped dried apricots

1 cup skinned hazelnuts, toasted and chopped

1/2 cup semisweet chocolate chips

Chocolate Cake
with Panforte Spices

I LOVE THE COMBINATION of cocoa, nuts, dried fruit, and spices in panforte, the long-keeping Italian fruitcake. So I thought I'd borrow them and put them in a dense chocolate cake and see what happened. The result isn't quite as long-keeping as panforte (which stays good for months!), but it has all the flavor appeal of the traditional cake in the form of a brownie.

1. Preheat the oven to 350°F. Grease a 9-inch round cake pan and dust with cocoa powder. Combine the flour, baking powder, salt, cinnamon, coriander, cloves, and nutmeg in a medium bowl.

2. Combine the butter and cocoa powder in a small saucepan and heat over medium-low heat until the butter is melted, whisking until smooth. Remove from the heat.

3. Combine the eggs and sugar in a large mixing bowl and beat with an electric mixer on high speed until thick and pale, about 5 minutes. With the mixer on low speed, stir in the butter mixture and hot water. Scrape down the sides of the bowl. With the mixer on low speed, stir in the flour mixture. Stir in the apricots, nuts, and chocolate chips.

4. Scrape the batter into the prepared pan and smooth with a rubber spatula. Bake until the cake is set and a toothpick inserted into the center of the cake comes out with just a few moist crumbs, about 30 to 40 minutes. Cool for 15 minutes. Run a sharp paring knife around the edges of the pan and invert the cake onto a cutting board. Re-invert onto a wire rack and cool completely. Slice and serve.

5. Store uneaten cake in a cake keeper or wrap in plastic and store at room temperature for up to 5 days.

Cornmeal-Almond Cake

THIS SIMPLE CAKE has a sandy but delicate texture and wholesome flavor from the cornmeal. It's great on its own, in the afternoon with a cup of tea, but it's also a wonderful partner with almost any kind of fresh fruit, from juicy orange sections in the winter to mixed raspberries, blackberries, and blueberries in the summer. Instead of whipped cream, try garnishing the cake and fruit with dollops of mascarpone.

1. Preheat the oven to 350°F. Grease a 9-inch round cake pan and dust with flour. Combine the cornmeal, flour, baking powder, and salt in a medium bowl. Combine 2/3 cup almonds and 1/4 cup sugar in the bowl of a food processor and finely grind. Whisk the almond mixture into the flour mixture.

2. Combine the butter and remaining 1/2 cup sugar in a large mixing bowl and cream with an electric mixer on medium-high speed until fluffy, about 3 minutes, scraping down the sides of the bowl once or twice as necessary. With the mixer on medium-low speed, add the eggs, one at a time, scraping down the sides of the bowl after each addition. Stir in the vanilla and almond extracts.

3. Turn the mixer to low and add the flour, 1/2 cup at a time, scraping down the sides of the bowl after each addition.

4. Scrape the batter into the prepared pan and smooth the top with a rubber spatula. Sprinkle with the remaining 1/3 cup sliced almonds. Bake until the cake is golden brown and a toothpick inserted into the center comes out clean, about 35 minutes. Let the cake cool in the pan for about 10 minutes, invert it onto a wire rack, and then turn it right side up on a rack to cool completely.

5. Dust with confectioners' sugar before slicing and serving.

6. Store uneaten cake in a cake keeper or wrap in plastic and store at room temperature for up to 2 days.

Serves 8

- 3/4 cup yellow cornmeal
- 1/4 cup unbleached all-purpose flour
- 1 teaspoon baking powder
- 1/2 teaspoon salt
- 1 cup sliced almonds
- 3/4 cup sugar
- 10 tablespoons (1 1/4 sticks) unsalted butter, softened
- 3 large eggs
- 1 teaspoon pure vanilla extract
- 1/2 teaspoon almond extract
- Confectioners' sugar for dusting

FOR THE CAKE

1¼ cups unbleached all-purpose flour

1½ teaspoons baking powder

¼ teaspoon salt

¾ cup (1½ sticks) unsalted butter, softened

1½ cups sugar

5 large eggs

1 teaspoon pure vanilla extract

¼ teaspoon coconut extract (optional)

¾ cup cream of coconut, such as Coco Lopez®

FOR THE GLAZE

¾ cup cream of coconut, such as Coco Lopez

3 tablespoons unsweetened Dutch process cocoa powder

Cream of Coconut Cake with Chocolate-Coconut Glaze

ONE 15-OUNCE CAN of cream of coconut is just enough to make this simple, rich cake and glaze. Use coconut extract in the cake if you like a strong coconut flavor, or leave it out if you want a more subtly perfumed coconut cake.

MAKE THE CAKE

1. Preheat the oven to 350°F. Grease a 9-inch round cake pan and dust with flour. Combine the flour, baking powder, and salt in a medium bowl.

2. Combine the butter and sugar in a large mixing bowl and cream with an electric mixer on medium-high speed until fluffy, about 3 minutes, scraping down the sides of the bowl once or twice as necessary. With the mixer on medium-low speed, add the eggs, one at a time, scraping down the sides of the bowl after each addition. Stir in the vanilla and coconut extract (if you are adding it).

3. Turn the mixer to low speed and add half of the flour mixture. Stir in the cream of coconut. Stir in the remaining flour mixture until just combined.

4. Scrape the batter into the prepared pan and smooth the top with a rubber spatula. Bake until the cake is golden brown and a toothpick inserted into the center comes out clean, 45 to 55 minutes. Let the cake cool in the pan for about 10 minutes; invert it onto a wire rack to cool completely.

MAKE THE GLAZE

1. Whisk together the cream of coconut and cocoa until smooth. Place the cake, still on the rack, on a rimmed baking sheet. Pour the glaze over the cake, letting it drip down the sides.

2. Store uneaten cake in a cake keeper or wrap in plastic and store at room temperature for up to 2 days.

- 2 cups unbleached all-purpose flour
- 1 1/4 cups sugar
- 1 teaspoon baking powder
- 1/4 teaspoon baking soda
- 1/4 teaspoon salt
- 1 cup plain whole-milk yogurt or lowfat yogurt
- 1/3 cup vegetable oil
- 2 large eggs
- 2 teaspoons pure vanilla extract
- Confectioners' sugar

Everyday Yogurt Cake

ASIDE FROM THE FACT that I always have the ingredients for this cake on hand, I often turn to this recipe because of its light and airy texture and straightforward flavor, perfect for when everyone in my family is craving "just plain cake." Although its name isn't very glamorous, it can be dressed up in a hundred different ways. One of my favorites: Place a paper doily on top before dusting it with confectioners' sugar to create a lacy decoration, and serve with sliced seasonal fresh fruit and yogurt on the side.

1. Preheat the oven to 350°F. Grease the bottom and sides of a 9-inch round cake pan and dust it with flour, knocking out any extra. Whisk together the flour, sugar, baking powder, baking soda, and salt in a large mixing bowl. Whisk together the yogurt, oil, eggs, and vanilla in a medium mixing bowl. Pour the yogurt mixture into the flour mixture and stir until just moistened.

2. Scrape the batter into the prepared pan and bake until the top of the cake is light golden and a toothpick inserted into the center is clean, about 40 minutes.

3. Let the cake cool in the pan for about 5 minutes, invert it onto a wire rack, and then turn it right side up on a rack to cool completely. Dust with confectioners' sugar, then slice and serve.

4. Store uneaten cake in a cake keeper or wrap in plastic and store at room temperature for up to 2 days.

Fig and Cornmeal Cake

DURING THE HOLIDAYS, my husband makes my favorite winter snack—dried figs stuffed with nuts and a few fennel seeds. Inspired by this snack, my Fig and Cornmeal Cake is simple but exotically flavored. I use pine nuts to give the cake an Italian flavor, but walnuts would be just as good.

1. Preheat the oven to 350°F. Grease a 9-inch round cake pan and dust it with flour, knocking out any extra. Combine the flour, cornmeal, baking powder, baking soda, and salt in a medium mixing bowl.

2. Combine the butter and sugar in a large mixing bowl and cream with an electric mixer on medium-high speed until fluffy, about 3 minutes, scraping down the sides of the bowl once or twice as necessary.

3. With the mixer on low speed, beat the eggs in, one at a time, scraping down the sides of the bowl after each addition. Stir in the orange zest and yogurt. Stir in the flour mixture, $1/2$ cup at a time, until just incorporated. Stir in the figs, pine nuts, and fennel seeds.

4. Scrape the batter into the prepared pan and smooth the top with a rubber spatula. Bake the cake until it is golden and a toothpick inserted into the center comes out clean, 35 to 40 minutes. Let the cake cool in the pan for about 5 minutes, invert it onto a wire rack, then turn it right side up on a rack to cool completely. Slice and serve.

5. Store uneaten cake in a cake keeper or wrap in plastic and store at room temperature for up to 2 days.

1 cup unbleached all-purpose flour

$1/2$ cup yellow cornmeal

1 teaspoon baking powder

$1/4$ teaspoon baking soda

$1/2$ teaspoon salt

$1/2$ cup (1 stick) unsalted butter, softened

1 cup sugar

2 large eggs, room temperature

$1/2$ teaspoon grated orange zest

$1/2$ cup lowfat or whole milk yogurt, room temperature

12 dried Calmyrna figs, tough stems removed, coarsely chopped

$1/3$ cup pine nuts, toasted and cooled

1 tablespoon fennel seeds

FOR THE CAKE

1½ cups unbleached all-purpose flour

1 teaspoon cinnamon

1 teaspoon baking powder

¼ teaspoon salt

½ cup (1 stick) unsalted butter, softened

1¼ cups sugar

3 large eggs, room temperature

1 tablespoon pear brandy or unflavored brandy

⅓ cup milk

1 ripe Anjou pear, peeled, cored, and cut into ⅓-inch pieces

½ cup raisins

½ cup toasted walnuts, chopped

FOR THE SAUCE

¾ cup sugar

½ cup water

½ cup plus 2 tablespoons heavy cream

5 tablespoons unsalted butter

1 teaspoon fleur de sel or other good-quality sea salt

Pear Cake
with Sea Salt–Caramel Sauce

I AM A FIEND for sea salt caramel, so I knew I had to include a cake with this type of sauce as an accompaniment. This rustic pear cake is just right served with vanilla ice cream and the warm sauce.

MAKE THE CAKE

1. Preheat the oven to 350°F. Grease a 9-inch round cake pan and dust it with flour. Combine the flour, cinnamon, baking powder, and salt in a medium mixing bowl.

2. Combine the butter and sugar in a large mixing bowl and cream with an electric mixer on medium-high speed until fluffy, about 3 minutes.

3. With the mixer on low speed, beat the eggs in, one at a time, scraping down the sides of the bowl after each addition. Stir in the brandy. Stir in ⅓ of the flour mixture until just incorporated. Stir in half the milk. Repeat, ending with the flour mixture and stirring on low until just combined. Stir in the pear, raisins, and nuts.

4. Scrape the batter into the prepared pan and smooth the top with a rubber spatula. Bake until a toothpick inserted in the center comes out clean, 45 to 50 minutes. Let the cake cool in the pan for about 5 minutes, invert it onto a wire rack, and then turn it right side up on a rack to cool completely.

MAKE THE SAUCE

1. Combine the sugar and water in a small, heavy saucepan. Bring to a boil. Continue to boil the mixture until it turns a light amber color. Do not stir. If part of the syrup is turning darker than the rest, gently tilt the pan to even out the cooking.

2. When the syrup is a uniform amber color, stir in the heavy cream with a long-handled wooden spoon. When the bubbling has subsided, remove the pot from the heat and stir in the butter and salt until the butter is melted. Transfer to a large heatproof measuring cup and let cool to warm before using.

3. Cut the cake into wedges, and serve with sauce on the side. Store leftover cake in a cake keeper or wrap in plastic and store at room temperature for up to 3 days.

1$\frac{1}{2}$ cups walnut pieces

$\frac{1}{3}$ cup sugar

1 cup unbleached all-purpose flour

1$\frac{1}{2}$ teaspoons baking powder

$\frac{1}{4}$ teaspoon salt

$\frac{3}{4}$ cup (1$\frac{1}{2}$ sticks) unsalted butter, softened

6 tablespoons honey

3 large eggs

1 teaspoon grated lemon zest

$\frac{1}{2}$ teaspoon pure vanilla extract

Confectioners' sugar

Honey *and* Walnut Cake

THIS IS A DELICIOUS, moist, rich cake with the beautiful fragrance of honey. Take care to tent it with foil after 25 minutes in the oven. Honey burns more quickly than sugar, so the surface of the cake should be shielded from overbrowning while the center bakes through.

1. Preheat the oven to 350°F. Grease a 9-inch round cake pan. Line the bottom of the pan with a circle of parchment paper. Grease the parchment. Dust the pan sides and parchment with flour. Spread the walnuts in a single layer on a baking sheet and toast until fragrant, 8 to 10 minutes. Let cool completely.

2. Combine the cooled walnuts and 1 tablespoon of sugar in the bowl of a food processor and process until the nuts are finely ground. Add the flour, baking powder, and salt and pulse to combine.

3. Add the butter, honey, and remaining sugar to the large mixing bowl and beat on medium-high speed until smooth, about 2 minutes, scraping down the sides of the bowl once or twice as necessary. Beat in the eggs, one at a time, scraping down the sides of the bowl after each addition. Beat in the zest and vanilla. Add the nut and flour mixture, $\frac{1}{2}$ cup at a time, and mix until just incorporated.

4. Scrape the batter into the prepared pan and smooth with a spatula. Bake until a toothpick inserted into the center of the cake comes out dry, 35 to 40 minutes. If the cake starts to brown too much around the edges, loosely tent it with foil after about 25 minutes.

5. Let the cake cool in the pan for 10 minutes, invert it onto a wire rack, and then turn it right side up again to cool completely. Dust heavily with confectioners' sugar before cutting into wedges and serving.

6. Store uneaten cake in a cake keeper or wrap in plastic and store at room temperature for up to 3 days.

Zebra Cake

I'D SEEN VERSIONS of this graphically striped cake all over the Internet and was dying to make a cake with the same effect. The technique is quite easy and well worth the few extra minutes it takes. Divide a batch of vanilla cake batter in two, coloring half of it with cocoa powder (use Dutch process, which is darker than natural cocoa, for the most striking chocolate-and-vanilla effect). Then, spoon alternating portions of vanilla and chocolate into the center of the pan. The batter layers will slowly spread out under the weight of the new layers, creating the zebra effect.

1. Preheat the oven to 350°F. Grease a 9-inch round cake pan, line with a circle of parchment paper, grease the parchment, and dust with flour. Combine the flour, baking powder, and salt in a medium bowl.

2. Combine the eggs and sugar in a large mixing bowl and beat with an electric mixer on high speed until thick and pale, about 5 minutes. With the mixer on low speed, stir in the milk, butter, vegetable oil, and vanilla, scraping down the sides of the bowl once or twice as necessary. Stir in the flour mixture 1/2 cup at a time.

3. Transfer 1/3 of the batter into another bowl and whisk in the cocoa powder.

4. Place 1/4 cup of the vanilla batter into the center of the pan and let it stand for a few seconds so it spreads out slightly. Place 2 tablespoons of the chocolate batter right on top of the vanilla and wait another few seconds until it spreads. Continue, alternating vanilla and chocolate, until you have used up all of the batter and it has spread to the edges of the pan.

5. Bake until the cake is set and a toothpick inserted into the center of the cake comes out clean, about 40 minutes. Cool in the pan for 10 minutes. Run a sharp paring knife around the edges of the pan and invert the cake onto a cutting board. Peel away the parchment paper. Re-invert onto a wire rack and cool completely. Slice and serve.

6. Store uneaten cake in a cake keeper or wrap in plastic and store at room temperature for up to 3 days.

Serves 8

2 cups unbleached all-purpose flour

1 tablespoon baking powder

1/4 teaspoon salt

4 large eggs

1 cup sugar

1 cup whole or 2% milk

1/2 cup (1 stick) butter, melted and cooled

1/2 cup vegetable oil

2 teaspoons pure vanilla extract

2 tablespoons unsweetened Dutch process cocoa powder

FOR THE TOPPING

6 tablespoons (³/₄ stick) unsalted butter

2 medium Granny Smith apples, peeled, cored, and cut into thin slices

²/₃ cup packed light brown sugar

3 tablespoons pure maple syrup

¹/₄ cup walnut pieces, toasted, cooled, and finely chopped

FOR THE CAKE

1¹/₂ cups unbleached all-purpose flour

2 teaspoons baking powder

¹/₂ teaspoon ground cinnamon

¹/₄ teaspoon salt

¹/₂ cup (1 stick) unsalted butter, softened

³/₄ cup granulated sugar

2 large eggs

1 teaspoon pure vanilla extract

¹/₂ cup milk

Apple-Walnut Upside-Down Cake

MAPLE SYRUP GIVES THE CARAMEL on this upside-down cake a seasonal flavor. Precooking the apples helps concentrate their flavor and gets rid of excess moisture.

MAKE THE TOPPING

1. Preheat the oven to 350°F. Grease a 9-inch round nonstick cake pan and dust with flour.

2. Heat 1 tablespoon butter in a large skillet over medium-high heat. Add the apples and cook until they begin to brown and soften, stirring frequently, about 5 minutes. Set aside to cool.

3. Heat the remaining 5 tablespoons of butter in a medium saucepan over medium heat until foaming. Stir in the brown sugar, turn the heat to medium-low, and cook, whisking, for 2 minutes. Scrape the mixture into the prepared pan and smooth with a spatula. Drizzle the maple syrup over the sugar mixture. Sprinkle the nuts evenly over the sugar. Arrange the apple slices in concentric circles on top of the sugar mixture. Set aside.

MAKE THE CAKE

1. Combine the flour, baking powder, cinnamon, and salt in a medium mixing bowl.

2. Combine the butter and granulated sugar in a large mixing bowl and cream with an electric mixer on medium-high speed until fluffy, about 3 minutes, scraping down the sides of the bowl once or twice as necessary. With the mixer on low, add the eggs, one at a time, scraping down the sides of the bowl after each addition. When the eggs have been added, turn the mixer to high speed and beat until the mixture is light and increased in volume, about 2 minutes. Stir in the vanilla.

3. With the mixer on low speed, stir in ¹/₃ of the flour mixture. Stir in ¹/₂ of the milk. Repeat with the remaining flour and milk, ending with the flour. Scrape down the sides of the bowl and beat the batter on high speed for 30 seconds.

4. Pour the batter over the apples, gently spreading it into an even layer with a spatula.

5. Bake until the cake is golden and a toothpick inserted into the center comes out clean, 35 to 40 minutes. Transfer the pan to a wire rack and let stand for 5 minutes.

6. Holding the pan and a plate together firmly with oven mitts, immediately invert the hot cake onto the plate. If necessary, replace any fruit stuck to the bottom of the pan. Let the cake cool for 20 minutes and serve warm, or serve at room temperature.

7. Store uneaten cake in a cake keeper at room temperature, or wrap loosely in plastic and store at room temperature for up to 2 days.

FOR THE TOPPING

1/2 cup (1 stick) unsalted butter

3/4 cup packed light brown sugar

3 ripe bananas, peeled and cut into 1/4-inch-thick slices

FOR THE CAKE

3/4 cup plus 2 table-spoons unbleached all-purpose flour

6 tablespoons unsweetened Dutch process cocoa powder, sifted

3/4 teaspoon baking soda

1/4 teaspoon salt

6 tablespoons (3/4 stick) unsalted butter, softened

1 cup granulated sugar

2 large eggs

2 teaspoons pure vanilla extract

2/3 cup buttermilk

Chocolate-Caramel-Banana Upside-Down Cake

THERE'S NO BETTER TOPPING for a dark chocolate cake than sweet bananas and gooey caramel. Serve this warm with vanilla ice cream and watch your guests swoon.

MAKE THE TOPPING

1. Preheat the oven to 350°F. Grease a 9-inch round nonstick pan and dust with flour.

2. Heat the butter in a medium saucepan over medium heat until foaming. Whisk in the brown sugar, turn the heat to low, and cook, whisking, for 2 minutes. Scrape the mixture into the prepared pan and smooth with a spatula. Arrange the banana slices in concentric circles on top of the sugar mixture. Set aside.

MAKE THE CAKE

1. Combine the flour, cocoa powder, baking soda, and salt in a medium mixing bowl.

2. Combine the butter and granulated sugar in a large mixing bowl and cream with an electric mixer on medium-high speed until fluffy, about 3 minutes.

3. With the mixer on low speed, add the eggs, one at a time, scraping down the sides after each. Turn the mixer to high speed and beat until the mixture is light and increased in volume, about 2 minutes. Stir in the vanilla.

4. With the mixer on low, stir in 1/3 of the flour mixture. Stir in 1/2 of the buttermilk. Repeat with the remaining flour and milk, ending with the flour. Scrape down the sides of the bowl and beat the batter on high speed for 30 seconds.

5. Pour the batter over the bananas, gently spreading it into an even layer.

6. Bake until a toothpick inserted into the center comes out clean, 40 to 45 minutes. Transfer the pan to a wire rack and let stand for 5 minutes. Holding the pan and a plate together with oven mitts, immediately invert the hot cake onto the plate. If necessary, replace any fruit stuck to the bottom of the pan. Let the cake cool for 20 minutes and serve warm, or serve at room temperature. Store uneaten cake in a cake keeper, or wrap in plastic and store at room temperature for up to 2 days.

FOR THE TOPPING

1 jar (24 ounces) sour cherries

6 tablespoons (¾ stick) unsalted butter

¼ cup packed light brown sugar

FOR THE CAKE

10 tablespoons unbleached all-purpose flour

1 teaspoon baking powder

½ cup yellow cornmeal

¼ teaspoon salt

6 tablespoons (¾ stick) unsalted butter, softened

¼ cup almond paste, crumbled

¾ cup granulated sugar

3 large eggs, at room temperature

1 teaspoon pure vanilla extract

½ teaspoon almond extract

½ cup milk

Cherry-Cornmeal Upside-Down Cake

FRESH SOUR CHERRIES are ideal for baking, but since they are only available where they are grown, it's more practical to plan on using jarred sour cherries, either domestic or imported (the ones in my supermarket come from Germany and are perfect for this purpose). Cornmeal and almond paste in the cake batter give it wonderful texture, color, and flavor.

MAKE THE TOPPING

1. Preheat the oven to 350°F. Grease a 9-inch round nonstick cake pan and dust with flour.

2. Place the cherries in a colander set over a bowl and let drain for 30 minutes, shaking the colander often. Combine the butter and brown sugar in a medium saucepan and heat over medium until the sugar is melted. Stir in the cherries, increase the heat to medium-high, and bring just to a boil. The cherries should be soft but still maintain their shape. Use a slotted spoon to transfer the cherries to a baking sheet to cool. Set aside the pan with the sugar mixture.

3. Arrange the cherries in the bottom of the prepared pan. Bring the sugar mixture back to a boil over medium-high heat, cook it without stirring for 3 minutes, and pour it over the cherries.

MAKE THE CAKE

1. Combine the flour, baking powder, cornmeal, and salt in a medium mixing bowl.

2. Combine the butter, almond paste, and granulated sugar in a large mixing bowl and cream with an electric mixer on medium-high speed until fluffy, about 3 minutes, scraping down the sides of the bowl once or twice as necessary. With the mixer on low speed, add the eggs, one at a time, scraping down the sides of the bowl after each addition. When all the eggs have been added, turn the mixer to high speed and beat until the mixture is light and increased in volume, about 2 minutes. Stir in the vanilla and almond extracts.

continued on page 62

continued from page 60

3. With the mixer on low speed, stir in ⅓ of the flour mixture. Stir in ½ of the milk. Repeat with the remaining flour and milk, ending with the flour. Scrape down the sides of the bowl and beat the batter on high speed for 30 seconds.

4. Pour the batter over the cherries, gently spreading it into an even layer with a spatula.

5. Bake until the cake is golden and a toothpick inserted into the center comes out clean, 35 to 40 minutes. Transfer the pan to a wire rack and let stand for 5 minutes.

6. Holding the pan and a plate together firmly with oven mitts, immediately invert the hot cake onto the plate. If necessary, replace any fruit stuck to the bottom of the pan. Let the cake cool for 20 minutes and serve warm, or serve at room temperature.

7. Store uneaten cake in a cake keeper at room temperature, or wrap loosely in plastic and store at room temperature for up to 2 days.

Mango Upside-Down Cake

IF, INSTEAD OF CANNED PINEAPPLE, you'd like to use fresh tropical fruit for your upside-down cake, consider mango, which is absolutely delicious as a cake topping when combined with rum, coconut, and chopped macadamias.

MAKE THE TOPPING

1. Preheat the oven to 350°F. Grease a 9-inch round nonstick cake pan and dust with flour.

2. Heat the butter in a medium saucepan over medium heat until foaming. Whisk in the brown sugar, turn the heat to low, and cook, whisking, for 2 minutes. Stir in the rum. Scrape the mixture into the prepared pan and tilt to cover the bottom of the pan. Sprinkle the coconut and macadamia nuts over the sugar mixture. Arrange the mango slices on top. Set aside.

MAKE THE CAKE

1. Combine the flour, baking powder, and salt in a medium mixing bowl.

2. In a large mixing bowl, beat the egg whites with an electric mixer until they just hold stiff peaks. Transfer to another bowl.

3. Place the egg yolks and granulated sugar in the large mixing bowl (no need to wash it) and beat on medium-high speed until pale yellow and increased in volume, about 5 minutes. Mix in the lime zest, milk, and vanilla. Stir in the flour mixture until smooth. Gently fold the whipped egg whites into the batter.

4. Pour the batter over the mangoes, gently spreading it into an even layer with a spatula.

5. Bake until the cake is golden and a toothpick inserted into the center comes out clean, 40 to 45 minutes. Transfer the pan to a wire rack and let stand for 5 minutes.

6. Holding the pan and a plate together firmly with oven mitts, immediately invert the hot cake onto the plate. If necessary, replace any fruit stuck to the bottom of the pan. Let the cake cool for 20 minutes and serve warm, or serve at room temperature.

7. Store uneaten cake in a cake keeper at room temperature, or wrap loosely in plastic and store at room temperature for up to 2 days.

Serves 8

FOR THE TOPPING

1/2 cup (1 stick) unsalted butter

3/4 cup packed dark brown sugar

2 tablespoons dark rum

1/3 cup sweetened flaked coconut

1/3 cup unsalted macadamia nuts, finely chopped

2 medium mangoes, peeled, pitted, and thinly sliced

FOR THE CAKE

1 cup unbleached all-purpose flour

1 teaspoon baking powder

1/4 teaspoon salt

3 large eggs, separated

1 cup granulated sugar

1 teaspoon grated lime zest

6 tablespoons milk

1 teaspoon pure vanilla extract

FOR THE TOPPING

1 cup sliced almonds

6 tablespoons ($3/4$ stick) unsalted butter

$2/3$ cup packed light brown sugar

$1/4$ cup honey

FOR THE CAKE

$1 1/2$ cups unbleached all-purpose flour

1 teaspoon baking powder

$1/2$ teaspoon baking soda

$1/4$ teaspoon salt

$1/2$ cup sour cream

2 large eggs

$1/4$ cup orange juice

1 teaspoon pure vanilla extract

$1/2$ cup (1 stick) unsalted butter, softened

$3/4$ cup granulated sugar

1 tablespoon grated orange zest

Orange-Almond-Caramel Upside-Down Cake

IN THIS STICKIEST of all upside-down cakes, the topping consists of a candy-like mixture of almonds, sugar, and honey, with no fruit. Line your pan with a circle of parchment paper and grease the parchment, even if your pan is nonstick, for an easy release after baking.

MAKE THE TOPPING

1. Preheat the oven to 350°F. Grease a 9-inch round nonstick cake pan and dust with flour. Line the bottom of the pan with a circle of parchment paper and grease and flour the parchment.

2. Spread the nuts on a baking sheet and toast until golden, 8 to 10 minutes. Heat the butter in a medium saucepan over medium heat until foaming. Whisk in the brown sugar, turn the heat to low, and cook, whisking, for 2 minutes. Scrape the mixture into the prepared pan and smooth with a spatula. Drizzle with the honey. Scatter the toasted almonds over the honey. Set aside.

MAKE THE CAKE

1. Combine the flour, baking powder, baking soda, and salt in a medium mixing bowl. Combine the sour cream, eggs, orange juice, and vanilla in a glass measuring cup and lightly beat.

2. Combine the butter and granulated sugar in a large mixing bowl and cream with an electric mixer on medium-high speed until fluffy, about 3 minutes, scraping down the sides of the bowl once or twice as necessary. Stir in the orange zest.

3. With the mixer on medium-low speed, pour the egg mixture into the bowl in a slow stream, stopping the mixer once or twice to scrape down the sides.

4. Turn the mixer to low speed and add the flour mixture, $1/2$ cup at a time, scraping down the sides of the bowl after each addition. After the last addition, mix for 30 seconds on medium speed.

5. Pour the batter over the almonds, gently spreading it into an even layer with a spatula.

6. Bake until the cake is golden and a toothpick inserted into the center comes out clean, 35 to 40 minutes. Transfer the pan to a wire rack and let stand for 5 minutes.

7. Holding the pan and a plate together firmly with oven mitts, immediately invert the hot cake onto the plate. Peel away the parchment paper. If necessary, replace any almonds stuck to the bottom of the pan. Let the cake cool for 20 minutes and serve warm, or serve at room temperature.

8. Store uneaten cake in a cake keeper at room temperature, or wrap loosely in plastic and store at room temperature for up to 2 days.

FOR THE TOPPING

1/2 cup (1 stick) unsalted butter

3/4 cup packed light brown sugar

2 large peaches, peeled and cut into 1/2-inch-thick slices

FOR THE CAKE

1 3/4 cups unbleached all-purpose flour

1 1/2 teaspoons baking powder

1/2 teaspoon baking soda

1/4 teaspoon salt

2 large eggs

1 teaspoon pure vanilla extract

3/4 cup buttermilk

1/2 cup (1 stick) unsalted butter, softened

3/4 cup granulated sugar

Peach-Buttermilk Upside-Down Cake

FOR MY LATE-SUMMER upside-down cake, local peaches provide a delicious fruit topping. Nectarines or apricots may be substituted, depending on your preference.

MAKE THE TOPPING

1. Preheat the oven to 375°F. Grease a 9-inch round nonstick pan and dust with flour.

2. Heat the butter in a medium saucepan over medium heat until foaming. Stir in the brown sugar, turn the heat to low, and cook, whisking, for 2 minutes. Scrape the mixture into the prepared pan and smooth with a spatula. Arrange the peach slices in concentric circles on top of the sugar mixture. Set aside.

MAKE THE CAKE

1. Combine the flour, baking powder, baking soda, and salt in a bowl. Combine the eggs, vanilla, and buttermilk in a glass measuring cup and lightly beat.

2. Combine the butter and granulated sugar in a large mixing bowl and cream with an electric mixer on medium-high speed until fluffy, about 3 minutes, scraping down the sides of the bowl as necessary.

3. With the mixer on medium-low speed, pour the egg mixture into the bowl in a slow stream, stopping the mixer once or twice to scrape down the sides. Turn the mixer to low speed and add the flour mixture, 1/2 cup at a time, scraping down the sides. After the last addition, mix for 30 seconds on medium speed.

4. Pour the batter over the peach mixture, gently spreading evenly with a spatula.

5. Bake until the cake is golden and a toothpick inserted into the center comes out clean, 35 to 40 minutes. Transfer the pan to a wire rack and let stand for 5 minutes.

6. Holding the pan and a plate together with oven mitts, invert the cake onto the plate. If necessary, replace any fruit stuck to the pan. Let the cake cool for 20 minutes and serve warm, or serve at room temperature. Store uneaten cake in a cake keeper or wrap in plastic and store at room temperature for up to 2 days.

FOR THE TOPPING

4 tablespoons (1/2 stick) unsalted butter

2/3 cup packed light brown sugar

1 can (20 ounces) pineapple chunks in heavy syrup, drained, patted dry with paper towels

FOR THE CAKE

3/4 cup boiling water

1/2 cup dark molasses

1 teaspoon baking soda

1 1/4 cups unbleached all-purpose flour

1 teaspoon baking powder

1/4 teaspoon salt

2 teaspoons ground ginger

1/2 teaspoon ground cinnamon

4 tablespoons (1/2 stick) unsalted butter, softened

1/2 cup firmly packed light brown sugar

1 large egg yolk

Pineapple-Gingerbread Upside-Down Cake

I LOVE THE WAY spicy cake contrasts with the sweetness of pineapple in this dessert, a great choice for winter baking, when fresh fruit is hard to find.

MAKE THE TOPPING

1. Preheat the oven to 350°F. Grease a 9-inch round nonstick cake pan and dust with flour.

2. Heat the butter in a medium saucepan over medium heat until foaming. Stir in the brown sugar, turn the heat to low, and cook, whisking, for 2 minutes. Scrape the mixture into the prepared pan and tilt the pan back and forth to cover. Arrange the pineapple chunks in concentric circles on top of the sugar mixture. Set aside.

MAKE THE CAKE

1. Pour the boiling water into a glass measuring cup and stir in the molasses and baking soda. Set aside to cool. Combine the flour, baking powder, salt, ginger, and cinnamon in a medium bowl.

2. Combine the butter and brown sugar in a large mixing bowl and cream with an electric mixer on medium-high speed until fluffy, about 3 minutes. Add the egg yolk and beat until smooth, scraping down the sides of the bowl once or twice as necessary. Beat in half the molasses mixture on medium speed and then half the flour mixture. Scrape down the bowl and repeat with the remaining molasses mixture and the remaining flour mixture.

3. Pour the batter over the pineapple, gently spreading it into an even layer. Bake until the cake is set and a toothpick inserted into the center comes out clean, about 35 minutes. Transfer the pan to a wire rack and let stand for 5 minutes.

4. Holding the pan and a plate together firmly with oven mitts, invert the cake onto the plate. If necessary, replace any fruit stuck to the pan. Let the cake cool for 20 minutes and serve warm or at room temperature. Store uneaten cake in a cake keeper, or wrap loosely in plastic and store at room temperature for up to 2 days.

Classic Pineapple Upside-Down Cake

ALTHOUGH TRADITIONAL UPSIDE-DOWN CAKE RECIPES call for pineapple rings, I prefer chunks, which are less decorative but cover the sponge layer more efficiently.

MAKE THE TOPPING

1. Preheat the oven to 350°F. Grease a 9-inch round nonstick cake pan and dust with flour.

2. Heat the butter in a medium saucepan over medium heat until foaming. Whisk in the brown sugar, turn the heat to low, and cook, whisking, for 2 minutes. Scrape the mixture into the prepared pan and smooth with a spatula. Arrange the pineapple chunks on top of the sugar mixture. Set aside.

MAKE THE CAKE

1. Combine the flour, baking powder, and salt in a medium mixing bowl.

2. In a large mixing bowl, beat the egg whites with an electric mixer until they just hold stiff peaks. Transfer to another bowl.

3. Place the egg yolks and granulated sugar in the large mixing bowl (no need to wash it) and beat on medium-high speed until pale yellow and increased in volume, about 5 minutes. Mix in the lemon zest, milk, and vanilla. Stir in the flour mixture until smooth. Gently fold the whipped egg whites into the batter.

4. Pour the batter over the pineapple chunks, gently spreading it into an even layer.

5. Bake until the cake is golden and a toothpick inserted into the center comes out clean, 40 to 45 minutes. Transfer the pan to a wire rack and let stand for 5 minutes.

6. Holding the pan and a plate together firmly with oven mitts, immediately invert the hot cake onto the plate. If necessary, replace any fruit stuck to the bottom of the pan. Let the cake cool for 20 minutes and serve warm, or serve at room temperature.

7. Store uneaten cake in a cake keeper at room temperature, or wrap loosely in plastic and store at room temperature for up to 2 days.

Serves 8

FOR THE TOPPING

1/2 cup (1 stick) unsalted butter

3/4 cup packed dark brown sugar

1 can (20 ounces) pineapple chunks in heavy syrup, drained, patted dry with paper towels

FOR THE CAKE

1 cup unbleached all-purpose flour

1 teaspoon baking powder

1/4 teaspoon salt

3 large eggs, separated

1 cup granulated sugar

1 teaspoon grated lemon zest

6 tablespoons milk

1 teaspoon pure vanilla extract

FOR THE TOPPING

1/2 cup (1 stick) unsalted butter

3/4 cup packed light brown sugar

1/2 teaspoon ground ginger

5 medium plums, pitted, halved, and cut into 1/2-inch-thick slices

1/2 cup blueberries, washed and picked over

FOR THE CAKE

1 cup granulated sugar

1/2 cup pecans

1 3/4 cups unbleached all-purpose flour

1 teaspoon baking powder

1/2 teaspoon baking soda

1/4 teaspoon salt

Pinch nutmeg

1 cup sour cream

2 large eggs

1 1/2 teaspoons pure vanilla extract

5 tablespoons unsalted butter

Plum-Blueberry Upside-Down Cake

CAKE BATTER MADE with sour cream is a rich and delicious base for plums and blueberries. This is a particularly beautiful cake, bright purple with blasts of blue.

MAKE THE TOPPING

1. Preheat the oven to 350°F. Grease a 9-inch round nonstick cake pan and dust with flour.

2. Heat the butter in a medium saucepan over medium heat until foaming. Add the brown sugar, ginger, plums, and blueberries and cook, stirring frequently, until the sugar is dissolved and the fruit is coated, 4 to 5 minutes. Remove the pan from the heat. Use a slotted spoon to remove the plums to a baking pan to cool slightly, leaving the syrup in the skillet.

MAKE THE CAKE

1. Arrange the plum slices in the bottom of the prepared pan. Bring the sugar mixture back to a boil over medium-high heat, cook without stirring for 3 minutes, and pour it over the plums.

2. Combine 1/4 cup of the granulated sugar and the pecans in the bowl of a food processor and process until finely ground. Combine the flour, baking powder, baking soda, salt, nutmeg, and ground nuts in a medium mixing bowl. Combine the sour cream, eggs, and vanilla in a glass measuring cup and lightly beat.

3. Combine the butter and the remaining 3/4 cup granulated sugar in a large mixing bowl and cream with an electric mixer on medium-high speed until fluffy, about 3 minutes, scraping down the sides of the bowl once or twice as necessary.

4. With the mixer on medium-low speed, pour the sour cream mixture into the bowl in a slow stream, stopping the mixer once or twice to scrape down the sides.

5. Turn the mixer to low speed and add the flour mixture, 1/2 cup at a time, scraping down the sides of the bowl after each addition. After the last addition, mix for 30 seconds on medium speed.

6. Pour the batter over the plums and blueberries, gently spreading it into an even layer with a spatula.

7. Bake until the cake is golden and a toothpick inserted into the center comes out clean, 40 to 45 minutes. Transfer the pan to a wire rack and let stand for 5 minutes.

8. Holding the pan and a plate together firmly with oven mitts, immediately invert the hot cake onto the plate. If necessary, replace any fruit stuck to the bottom of the pan. Let the cake cool for 20 minutes and serve warm, or serve at room temperature.

9. Store uneaten cake in a cake keeper at room temperature, or wrap loosely in plastic and store at room temperature for up to 2 days.

CHAPTER 3
Loaf Cakes

*Chocolate-Raspberry Marble Pound Cake
with Chocolate-Raspberry Glaze*—recipe on page 78

I've always loved loaf cakes, but until now I've never attempted to analyze their appeal. After gazing upon a freshly baked Lavender and Lemon Pound Cake, admiring its golden glow, inhaling its heavenly scent, and, finally, slicing into it and gobbling up a piece, I'm able to list the qualities that make these cakes so attractive:

- Resembling a humble loaf of bread, this kind of cake conjures ideas of home-baked goodness. The best loaf cakes, chock full of butter, scented with vanilla, bursting with nuts, and filled with moist fruit, deliver on this promise.

- They don't cry out for frostings or glazes. In fact, I think they are more beautiful when unembellished, the better to admire the crunchy crevice that often runs from one end to the other, the result of the cake's volcanic rise in the oven.

- Because of their sturdy, compact shape, they are easy to pack up and carry to a friend's house, a bake sale, or a picnic. Thick slices, wrapped in plastic, can withstand the jostling inside a lunch box without crumbling.

- Loaf cakes, because of their shape, will generally stay fresh longer than flatter, thinner cakes. Wrapped in plastic and refrigerated, many of them will stay fresh for up to 5 days, although in my house, the last crumbs are gone before the 3 days they'll stay fresh at room temperature. If you are looking for a real keeper, this chapter is a good place to start.

- Even stale loaf cakes can be enjoyed days after baking, sliced and toasted in a toaster oven or on a baking sheet. A scoop of ice cream on top won't hurt.

Loaf cakes are thicker than cakes baked in round or square baking pans and more likely to be dense and heavy if their ingredients aren't handled properly. It's important to do everything you can to ensure their rise. Cream your butter and sugar together for the recommended time to whip adequate air into the butter. Room temperature butter will trap more air than cold butter when creamed together with sugar, resulting in a higher rise and a lighter cake. Eggs should also be at room temperature to guarantee a smooth, emulsified batter, which will also rise better than a grainy, lumpy mixture.

Grease the pan and then dust it with flour to ensure an easy release. Most loaf cakes will slide right out of the pan, but it doesn't hurt to run a paring knife around the edges of the pan to make sure any sticky ingredients are loosened.

Thicker cakes take longer to set up once they are out of the oven than thinner ones. Loaf cakes should be cooled in the pan for 5 minutes or so before being inverted onto a wire rack to cool completely. This time in the pan will make them sturdier and less likely to fall apart.

It may be tempting to cut into your loaf cake while it is still warm, but you will get neater slices if you wait until the cake is completely cooled. Use a serrated knife and a sawing motion to cut through your cooled loaf. Be generous—slices at least $\frac{1}{2}$ inch thick are less likely to fall apart than super-skinny ones.

Brown Sugar Pound Cake
with Raisins

BROWN SUGAR GIVES this pound cake a bit of molasses flavor and a wonderfully moist crumb. It's a great breakfast or brunch cake, but it can serve beautifully as dessert when paired with vanilla ice cream and caramel sauce.

1. Preheat the oven to 325°F. Grease a 9-inch by 5-inch loaf pan and dust with flour.

2. Combine the buttermilk, eggs, and vanilla in a glass measuring cup and lightly beat. Toss the raisins with 1 tablespoon of flour and set aside. Combine the remaining flour, baking powder, baking soda, and salt in a medium mixing bowl.

3. Combine the butter and brown sugar in a large mixing bowl and cream with an electric mixer on medium-high speed until fluffy, about 3 minutes, scraping down the sides of the bowl once or twice as necessary.

4. With the mixer on medium-low speed, pour the egg mixture into the bowl in a slow stream, stopping the mixer once or twice to scrape down the sides.

5. Turn the mixer to low speed and add the flour mixture, $1/2$ cup at a time, scraping down the sides of the bowl after each addition. After the last addition, mix for 30 seconds on medium speed. Stir in the raisins.

6. Scrape the batter into the prepared pan and smooth the top with a rubber spatula. Stir together the granulated sugar and cinnamon in a small bowl. Sprinkle over the top of the cake. Bake the cake until it is golden and a toothpick inserted in the center comes out clean, about 55 minutes. Let the cake cool in the pan for about 5 minutes, invert it onto a wire rack, and then turn it right side up on a rack to cool completely. Slice and serve.

7. Store uneaten cake in a cake keeper or wrap in plastic and store at room temperature for up to 3 days.

Serves 8 to 10

- ½ cup buttermilk
- 2 large eggs
- 1 teaspoon pure vanilla extract
- 1 cup raisins
- 1½ cups unbleached all-purpose flour
- 1 teaspoon baking powder
- ½ teaspoon baking soda
- ¼ teaspoon salt
- ½ cup (1 stick) unsalted butter, softened
- ¾ cup packed light brown sugar
- 2 tablespoons granulated sugar
- 1 teaspoon ground cinnamon

2 tablespoons anise seeds

1/3 cup sour cream

2 large eggs

1 large egg yolk

1 teaspoon pure vanilla extract

1 1/2 cups cake flour

3/4 teaspoons baking powder

1/4 teaspoon salt

3/4 cup (1 1/2 sticks) unsalted butter, softened

1 1/4 cup sugar

Anise Pound Cake

ANISE IS ONE OF MY favorite dessert flavors, and I try to bake with it whenever I can. Here, I toast and grind some of the seeds to intensify their flavor in pound cake. Slices of the fragrant cake are delicious when served with vanilla ice cream. Or make a dried fruit compote: Bring 1/2 pound of dried apricots, figs, and prunes to a boil with 1 1/4 cups of water and half of a split vanilla bean. Simmer until the fruit is softened and the liquid becomes syrupy, about 10 minutes.

1. Preheat the oven to 325°F. Grease a 9-inch by 5-inch loaf pan and dust with flour. Place the anise seeds in a small skillet and toast over medium heat until fragrant, 2 to 3 minutes. Transfer to a spice grinder and grind fine. Set aside.

2. Combine the sour cream, eggs, egg yolk, and vanilla in a glass measuring cup and lightly beat. Combine the flour, baking powder, and salt in a medium mixing bowl.

3. Combine the butter and sugar in a large mixing bowl and cream with an electric mixer on medium-high speed until fluffy, about 3 minutes, scraping down the sides of the bowl once or twice as necessary.

4. With the mixer on medium-low speed, pour the egg mixture into the bowl in a slow stream, stopping the mixer once or twice to scrape down the sides.

5. Turn the mixer to low speed and add the flour mixture, 1/2 cup at a time, scraping down the sides of the bowl after each addition. After the last addition, mix for 30 seconds on medium speed.

6. Scrape the batter into the prepared pan and smooth the top with a rubber spatula. Bake the cake until it is golden and a toothpick inserted in the center comes out clean, about 1 hour and 15 minutes. Let the cake cool in the pan for about 5 minutes, invert it onto a wire rack, and then turn it right side up on a rack to cool completely. Slice and serve.

7. Store uneaten cake in a cake keeper or wrap in plastic and store at room temperature for up to 3 days.

FOR THE CAKE

3 ounces semisweet or bittersweet chocolate, finely chopped

4 large eggs, at room temperature, lightly beaten

2 teaspoons pure vanilla extract

1½ cups cake flour

¾ teaspoon baking powder

¼ teaspoon salt

1 cup (2 sticks) unsalted butter, softened

1¼ cups sugar

¼ cup raspberry jam

FOR THE GLAZE

¼ cup raspberry jam

6 tablespoons heavy cream

2 tablespoons light corn syrup

4 ounces bittersweet chocolate

1 tablespoon raspberry liqueur

Chocolate-Raspberry Marble Pound Cake *with* Chocolate-Raspberry Glaze

HERE'S A FUN TWIST on marble pound cake. Some raspberry jam stirred into the vanilla portion of the batter gives the cake subtle fruit flavor, which naturally complements the chocolate. Coating the cake with more jam before glazing it with chocolate is an extra step, but only takes a few minutes and reinforces the flavor combination. The jam won't color the batter significantly, so add a drop or two of red food coloring to the raspberry batter for a more colorful cake if you like.

MAKE THE CAKE

1. Preheat the oven to 325°F. Grease a 9-inch by 5-inch loaf pan and dust with flour.

2. Put 1 inch of water in the bottom of a double boiler or a small saucepan and bring to a bare simmer. Place the chocolate in the top of the double boiler or in a stainless steel bowl big enough to rest on top of the saucepan, and set the bowl on top of the simmering water, making sure that the water doesn't touch the bottom of the bowl. Heat, whisking occasionally, until the chocolate is completely melted, 5 to 7 minutes. Set aside to cool.

3. Combine the eggs and vanilla in a glass measuring cup and lightly beat. Combine the flour, baking powder, and salt in a medium mixing bowl.

4. Combine the butter and sugar in a large mixing bowl and cream with an electric mixer on medium-high speed until fluffy, about 3 minutes, scraping down the sides of the bowl once or twice as necessary.

5. With the mixer on medium-low speed, pour the egg mixture into the bowl in a slow stream, stopping the mixer once or twice to scrape down the bowl.

continued on page 80

continued from page 78

6. Turn the mixer on low speed and add the flour mixture, $1/2$ cup at a time, scraping down the sides of the bowl after each addition. After the last addition, mix for 30 seconds on medium speed.

7. Scrape half the batter into a medium mixing bowl and whisk in the raspberry jam. Whisk the melted chocolate into the batter remaining in the mixer.

8. Scrape $1/2$ the raspberry batter into the prepared loaf pan and smooth the top, then add $1/2$ of the chocolate batter. Repeat the layers with the remaining batters. Run a butter knife blade through the batter to create marbling. Do not overmix.

9. Bake the pound cake until it is golden and a toothpick inserted in the center comes out clean, about 1 hour and 15 minutes. Let the cake cool in the pan for about 10 minutes, invert it onto a wire rack, and then turn it right side up on a rack to cool completely.

MAKE THE GLAZE

1. Heat $1/4$ cup raspberry jam until loose, and use a pastry brush to brush the warm jam all over the top and sides of the cake. Combine the heavy cream, corn syrup, and chocolate in a small pot and heat over medium, whisking until smooth. Stir in the raspberry liqueur. Let stand until thickened, about 30 minutes. Spoon the glaze over the cake, smoothing it over the top and sides with a small metal spatula to cover. Let stand until the glaze firms up, about 1 hour. Slice and serve.

2. Store uneaten cake in a cake keeper at room temperature, or wrap loosely in plastic and store at room temperature for up to 3 days.

Chocolate Cream Pound Cake

THIS LOAF CAKE IS MADE exceptionally tender by the addition of some heavy cream. It has a delicate texture and melts in the mouth. Because the cake is so crumbly, a slice is probably not the ideal choice for a lunch box, but definitely a treat if you are staying home.

1. Preheat the oven to 325°F. Grease a 9-inch by 5-inch loaf pan and dust with flour.

2. Sift the cocoa powder through a fine strainer and into a heatproof bowl. Place the cream in a microwave-safe measuring cup and heat until just boiling, 30 seconds to 1 minute depending on the power of your microwave. Pour the hot cream over the cocoa and stir and mash with a spoon to make a thick paste. Set aside to cool.

3. Combine the flour, baking soda, and salt in a medium mixing bowl.

4. Combine the butter and sugar in a large mixing bowl and cream with an electric mixer on medium-high speed until fluffy, about 3 minutes, scraping down the sides of the bowl once or twice as necessary. Beat in the cocoa powder paste until smooth.

5. With the mixer on medium-low speed, add the eggs, one at a time, scraping down the sides of the bowl after each addition. Stir in the vanilla.

6. Turn the mixer to low speed and add the flour mixture, $1/2$ cup at a time, scraping down the sides of the bowl after each addition. After the last addition, mix for 30 seconds on medium speed.

7. Scrape the batter into the prepared pan and smooth the top with a rubber spatula. Bake the cake until it is firm to the touch and a toothpick inserted in the center comes out clean, about 1 hour and 10 minutes. Let the cake cool in the pan for 5 minutes, invert it onto a wire rack, and then turn it right side up on a rack to cool completely. Slice and serve.

8. Store uneaten cake in a cake keeper or wrap in plastic and store at room temperature for up to 3 days.

Serves 8 to 10

6 tablespoons unsweetened Dutch process cocoa powder

$1/4$ cup heavy cream

1 cup plus 2 tablespoons unbleached all-purpose flour

$1/4$ teaspoon baking soda

$1/4$ teaspoon salt

$1/2$ cup (1 stick) unsalted butter, softened

$1 1/2$ cups sugar

3 large eggs

1 teaspoon pure vanilla extract

4 large eggs, at room temperature, lightly beaten

1 teaspoon pure vanilla extract

1½ cups cake flour

¾ teaspoon baking powder

1½ teaspoons ground black pepper

¼ teaspoon salt

1 cup (2 sticks) unsalted butter, softened

1¼ cups sugar

1 teaspoon grated orange zest

1 teaspoon grated lime zest

1 teaspoon grated lemon zest

Citrus and *Black Pepper* Pound Cake

CREAMING THE FRUIT ZEST with the butter and sugar helps to release the zest's oils, making for a wonderfully aromatic cake. Freshly ground black pepper gives it a bit of a bite. Serve thin slices with diced fresh pineapple, which marries well with the citrus and spice.

1. Preheat the oven to 325°F. Grease a 9-inch by 5-inch loaf pan and dust with flour.

2. Combine the eggs and vanilla in a glass measuring cup and lightly beat. Combine the flour, baking powder, black pepper, and salt in a medium mixing bowl.

3. Combine the butter, sugar, orange zest, lime zest, and lemon zest in a large mixing bowl and cream with an electric mixer on medium-high speed until fluffy, about 3 minutes, scraping down the sides of the bowl once or twice as necessary.

4. With the mixer on medium-low speed, pour the egg mixture into the bowl in a slow stream, stopping the mixer once or twice to scrape down the sides.

5. Turn the mixer to low speed and add the flour mixture, ½ cup at a time, scraping down the sides of the bowl after each addition. After the last addition, mix for 30 seconds on medium speed.

6. Scrape the batter into the prepared pan and smooth the top with a rubber spatula. Bake the cake until it is golden and a toothpick inserted in the center comes out clean, about 1 hour and 15 minutes. Let the cake cool in the pan for about 5 minutes, invert it onto a wire rack, and then turn it right side up on a rack to cool completely. Slice and serve.

7. Store uneaten cake in a cake keeper or wrap in plastic and store at room temperature for up to 3 days.

Orange Blossom Honey Pound Cake

ORANGE BLOSSOM HONEY sweetens this fragrant pound cake while orange zest gives it a mild orange flavor. Honey burns more quickly than sugar, so tent the cake with foil if you notice, during baking, that the top is browning more quickly than the cake underneath is baking.

1. Preheat the oven to 325°F. Grease the inside of a 9-inch by 5-inch loaf pan and dust with flour. Combine the flour, baking powder, and salt in a medium bowl.

2. Combine the butter, honey, and sugar in a large mixing bowl and cream with an electric mixer on medium-high speed until fluffy, about 3 minutes, scraping down the sides of the bowl one or twice as necessary. Beat in the eggs, one at a time, scraping down the sides of the bowl after each addition. Stir in the orange zest and vanilla.

3. With the mixer on low, add the flour mixture $1/2$ cup at a time, scraping down the sides of the bowl a few times as necessary. After the last addition, mix for 30 seconds on medium speed.

4. Scrape the batter into the prepared pan and smooth the top with a rubber spatula. Bake until the cake is golden brown and a toothpick inserted into the center comes out clean, 50 to 55 minutes. Check on the cake after about 40 minutes. If you notice that it is very brown, tent a sheet of aluminum foil over the top for the remainder of the baking. Let the cake cool in the pan for about 10 minutes, invert it onto a wire rack, and then turn it right side up on a rack to cool completely. Slice and serve.

5. Store uneaten cake in a cake keeper or wrap in plastic and store at room temperature for up to 3 days.

Serves 8 to 10

- 2$1/4$ cups unbleached all-purpose flour
- 1$1/2$ teaspoons baking powder
- $1/4$ teaspoon salt
- $3/4$ cup (1$1/2$ sticks) unsalted butter, softened
- 1 cup orange blossom honey
- 3 tablespoons sugar
- 2 large eggs
- 1 teaspoon grated orange zest
- 1 teaspoon pure vanilla extract

1 cup dried apricots, finely chopped

1 cup plus 1 tablespoon unbleached all-purpose flour

$1/2$ cup unsweetened Dutch process cocoa powder

$1^1/2$ teaspoons baking powder

$1/4$ teaspoon salt

$1/2$ teaspoon ground cinnamon

$1/8$ teaspoon ground cloves

$1/2$ cup (1 stick) unsalted butter, softened

$1^1/2$ cups sugar

3 large eggs

1 teaspoon pure vanilla extract

$1/2$ cup milk

Clove-Scented Chocolate and Apricot Loaf

JUST A SMALL AMOUNT of ground cloves gives this chocolate loaf a mysterious and complex flavor. Apricots add moisture, color, and a beautiful acidity that complements the chocolate and spice.

1. Preheat the oven to 325°F. Grease a 9-inch by 5-inch loaf pan and dust with flour.

2. Combine the apricots and 1 tablespoon of flour in a small bowl. Set aside. Whisk together the remaining 1 cup flour, cocoa powder, baking powder, salt, cinnamon, and cloves in a medium mixing bowl.

3. Combine the butter and sugar in a large mixing bowl and cream with an electric mixer on medium-high speed until fluffy, about 3 minutes, scraping down the sides of the bowl once or twice as necessary.

4. With the mixer on medium-low speed, add the eggs, one at a time, scraping down the sides of the bowl after each addition. Stir in the vanilla.

5. Turn the mixer to low speed and add $1/3$ of the flour mixture, then $1/2$ of the milk. Repeat, ending with the flour. After the last addition, mix for 1 minute on medium speed. Stir in the apricots.

6. Scrape the batter into the prepared pan and smooth the top with a rubber spatula. Bake the cake until it is firm to the touch and a toothpick inserted in the center comes out clean, about 1 hour and 10 minutes. Let the cake cool in the pan for 5 minutes, invert it onto a wire rack, and then turn it right side up on a rack to cool completely. Slice and serve.

7. Store uneaten cake in a cake keeper or wrap in plastic and store at room temperature for up to 3 days.

3/4 cup whole milk

1 tablespoon finely chopped fresh lavender leaves

1 3/4 cups unbleached all-purpose flour

1 1/4 teaspoons baking powder

1/4 teaspoon salt

1/2 cup (1 stick) unsalted butter, softened

1 cup sugar

1 tablespoon grated lemon zest

2 large eggs

Lavender and Lemon Pound Cake

STEEPING THE LAVENDER in milk infuses this cake with an intense and beautiful aroma. Serve with scoops of vanilla ice cream or with sliced strawberries and whipped cream.

1. Combine the milk and lavender in a small saucepan over medium heat. Bring just to a simmer, transfer to a glass measuring cup, and let cool to room temperature.

2. Preheat the oven to 325°F. Grease the inside of a 9-inch by 5-inch loaf pan and dust with flour. Combine the flour, baking powder, and salt in a medium bowl.

3. Combine the butter, sugar, and zest in a large mixing bowl and cream with an electric mixer on medium-high speed until fluffy, about 3 minutes, scraping down the sides of the bowl once or twice as necessary. Beat in the eggs, one at a time, scraping down the sides of the bowl after each addition.

4. With the mixer on low speed, add 1/3 of the flour mixture and mix until incorporated. Add 1/2 of the milk and mix until incorporated. Repeat with the remaining flour and milk, ending with the flour. After the last addition, mix for 30 seconds on medium speed.

5. Scrape the batter into the prepared pan and smooth the top with a rubber spatula. Bake until the cake is golden brown and a toothpick inserted into the center comes out clean, 50 to 55 minutes. Let the cake cool in the pan for about 10 minutes, invert it onto a wire rack, and then turn it right side up on a rack to cool completely. Slice and serve.

6. Store uneaten cake in a cake keeper or wrap in plastic and store at room temperature for up to 3 days.

FOR THE CAKE

1½ cups unbleached all-purpose flour

½ teaspoon baking powder

1 teaspoon baking soda

¼ teaspoon salt

½ cup (1 stick) unsalted butter, softened

¾ cup firmly packed brown sugar

2 large eggs

½ cup sour cream

1 tablespoon grated orange zest

1 teaspoon pure vanilla extract

1 cup semisweet chocolate chips

FOR THE GLAZE

2 tablespoons sour cream

¾ cup confectioners' sugar

½ teaspoon pure vanilla extract

Orange–Chocolate Chip Pound Cake with Sour Cream Glaze

I LOVE THE COMBINATION of orange and chocolate in this cake, which gets tenderness and a little more tang from sour cream. Don't skip the sour cream glaze, which adds an interesting layer of creaminess, making this simple cake a surprisingly complex combination of flavors and textures.

MAKE THE CAKE

1. Preheat the oven to 325°F. Grease the inside of a 9-inch by 5-inch loaf pan and dust with flour. Combine the flour, baking powder, baking soda, and salt in a medium bowl.

2. Combine the butter and brown sugar in a large mixing bowl and cream with an electric mixer on medium-high speed until fluffy, about 3 minutes, scraping down the sides of the bowl once or twice as necessary. Beat in the eggs, one at a time, scraping down the sides of the bowl after each addition. Beat in the sour cream. Stir in the orange zest and vanilla.

3. With the mixer on low, add the flour mixture ½ cup at a time, scraping down the sides of the bowl a few times as necessary. After the last addition, mix for 30 seconds on medium speed. Stir in the chocolate chips.

4. Scrape the batter into the prepared pan and smooth the top with a rubber spatula. Bake until the cake is golden brown and a toothpick inserted into the center comes out clean, 50 to 55 minutes. Let the cake cool in the pan for about 10 minutes, invert it onto a wire rack, and then turn it right side up on a rack to cool completely.

MAKE THE GLAZE

1. Whisk together the sour cream, confectioners' sugar, and vanilla. Spread the glaze over the top of the cake with an offset spatula, letting it drip down the sides. Let stand until the glaze is set, about 1 hour. Slice and serve.

2. Store uneaten cake in a cake keeper or loosely wrap in plastic and store at room temperature for up to 3 days.

Peanut Butter— Chocolate Chip Pound Cake

Serves 8 to 10

I LIKE THE WAY dark chocolate chips (try Ghirardelli® 60% Cacao Bittersweet Chocolate Chips) give this wonderfully moist pound cake a grown-up edge, but semisweet or even milk chocolate chips may be substituted for a more kid-pleasing version. If you can resist eating it straight from the cake keeper, try it toasted (melty chocolate chips!) with a scoop of vanilla ice cream.

1. Preheat the oven to 325°F. Grease a 9-inch by 5-inch loaf pan and dust with flour.

2. Combine the eggs and vanilla in a large glass measuring cup and lightly beat. Combine the flour, baking powder, and salt in a medium bowl.

3. Combine the butter, peanut butter, and brown sugar in a large mixing bowl and cream with an electric mixer on medium-high speed until fluffy, about 3 minutes, scraping down the sides of the bowl once or twice as necessary. With the mixer on medium-low speed, pour the egg mixture into the bowl in a slow stream, stopping once or twice to scrape down the sides of the bowl. Turn the mixer to low speed and add the flour, $1/2$ cup at a time, scraping down the sides of the bowl after each addition. After the last addition, mix on medium speed for 1 minute. Stir in the chocolate chips.

4. Scrape the batter into the prepared pan and smooth the top with a rubber spatula. Bake until the cake is golden brown and a toothpick inserted into the center comes out clean, about 1 hour and 20 minutes, tenting the cake with foil after about 1 hour if it looks like it is browning too quickly. Let the cake cool in the pan for about 10 minutes, invert it onto a wire rack, and then turn it right side up on a rack to cool completely. Slice and serve.

5. Store uneaten cake in a cake keeper or wrap in plastic and store at room temperature for up to 3 days.

Ingredients:

- 4 large eggs
- 2 teaspoons pure vanilla extract
- $1\frac{1}{2}$ cups unbleached all-purpose flour
- 1 teaspoon baking powder
- $1/4$ teaspoon salt
- $3/4$ cup ($1\frac{1}{2}$ sticks) unsalted butter, softened
- $1/2$ cup smooth peanut butter
- 1 cup packed light brown sugar
- 1 bag (12 ounces) bittersweet or semisweet chocolate chips

- 4 large eggs, at room temperature, lightly beaten
- 2 teaspoons pure vanilla extract
- 1½ cups unbleached all-purpose flour
- ¾ teaspoon baking powder
- ¼ teaspoon salt
- 1 cup (2 sticks) unsalted butter, softened
- 1¼ cups sugar
- 1 jar (13 ounces, about 1 cup) Nutella®

Nutella Swirl Pound Cake

HERE IS ONE OF THE EASIEST and best ways to incorporate Nutella into a cake. Just sandwich a small jar's worth of Nutella between layers of vanilla pound cake batter, swirl with a knife to marble, and bake. Strong coffee ice cream (I like all of the Starbucks® varieties) nicely complements the vanilla, chocolate, and hazelnut flavors.

1. Preheat the oven to 325°F. Grease a 9-inch by 5-inch loaf pan and dust with flour.

2. Combine the eggs and vanilla in a glass measuring cup and lightly beat. Combine the flour, baking powder, and salt in a medium mixing bowl.

3. Combine the butter and sugar in a large mixing bowl and cream with an electric mixer on medium-high speed until fluffy, about 3 minutes, scraping down the sides of the bowl once or twice as necessary.

4. With the mixer on medium-low speed, pour the egg mixture into the bowl in a slow stream, stopping the mixer once or twice to scrape down the sides.

5. Turn the mixer to low speed and add the flour mixture, ½ cup at a time, scraping down the sides of the bowl after each addition. After the last addition, mix for 30 seconds on medium speed.

6. Scrape ⅓ of the batter into the prepared pan and smooth with a spatula. Spread ½ of the Nutella over the batter and smooth with a cleaned spatula. Scrape another ⅓ of the batter over the Nutella and smooth. Scrape the remaining Nutella over the batter and smooth. Spread the remaining batter over the Nutella and smooth. Run a butter knife blade through the batter to create marbling. Do not overmix.

7. Bake the cake until it is golden and a toothpick inserted into the center comes out clean, about 1 hour and 15 minutes. Let the cake cool in the pan for 15 minutes, invert it onto a wire rack, and then turn it right side up on a rack to cool completely. Slice and serve.

8. Store uneaten cake in a cake keeper or wrap in plastic and store at room temperature for up to 3 days.

FOR THE CAKE

1³⁄₄ cups unbleached all-purpose flour

³⁄₄ teaspoon baking powder

¹⁄₄ teaspoon salt

4 large eggs

¹⁄₂ teaspoon maple extract

¹⁄₂ teaspoon pure vanilla extract

14 tablespoons (1³⁄₄ sticks) unsalted butter, softened

1 cup packed light brown sugar

5 tablespoons pure maple syrup

1 cup pecans, toasted, cooled, and chopped

FOR THE GLAZE

¹⁄₂ cup confectioners' sugar

2 tablespoons heavy cream

1 tablespoon maple syrup

1¹⁄₂ teaspoons fresh lemon juice

¹⁄₄ teaspoon maple extract

Maple-Pecan Pound Cake

I LIKE TO SERVE SLICES of this maple cake in the fall with fresh cranberries cooked in a little bit of maple syrup just until they've started to soften up and pop.

MAKE THE CAKE

1. Preheat the oven to 325°F. Grease a 9-inch by 5-inch loaf pan with cooking spray and dust it with flour. Whisk together the flour, baking powder, and salt in a medium bowl.

2. Combine the eggs, maple extract, and vanilla extract in a glass measuring cup and lightly beat.

3. Combine the butter and brown sugar in a large mixing bowl and cream with an electric mixer on medium-high speed until fluffy, about 3 minutes, scraping down the sides of the bowl once or twice as necessary. Stir in the maple syrup until smooth.

4. With the mixer on medium-low speed, pour the egg mixture into the bowl in a slow stream, stopping the mixer once or twice to scrape down the sides.

5. Turn the mixer to low speed and add the flour mixture, ¹⁄₂ cup at a time, scraping down the sides of the bowl after each addition. After the last addition, mix for 30 seconds. Stir in the pecans.

6. Scrape the batter into the prepared pan and smooth the top with a rubber spatula. Bake the cake until it is golden brown and a toothpick inserted in the center comes out clean, about 1 hour and 15 minutes. Let the cake cool in the pan for about 5 minutes, invert it onto a wire rack, and then turn it right side up on a rack to cool completely.

MAKE THE GLAZE

1. Combine the confectioners' sugar, cream, maple syrup, lemon juice, and maple extract in a medium bowl and whisk until smooth. Move the whisk back and forth across the cake, drizzling it over the top and letting it drip down the sides. Let stand until the glaze sets, about 1 hour. Slice and serve. Store uneaten cake in a cake keeper or loosely wrap in plastic and store at room temperature for up to 3 days.

Marble Molasses Pound Cake

Serves 8 to 10

THERE'S NO REASON TO CONFINE your marbling to chocolate and vanilla. Here, molasses colors and flavors some of the cake batter. I like the mild flavor of molasses on its own, but if you like a spicier, more gingerbread-like cake, add $1/2$ teaspoon of ginger and $1/2$ teaspoon of cinnamon to the molasses batter before marbling.

2 cups unbleached all-purpose flour

2 teaspoons baking powder

$1/4$ teaspoon salt

$1/2$ cup (1 stick) unsalted butter, softened

1 cup granulated sugar

2 large eggs

2 teaspoons pure vanilla extract

$2/3$ cup whole milk

$1/2$ cup pecans, toasted and finely chopped

3 tablespoons dark (not blackstrap) molasses

1 tablespoon dark corn syrup

$1/4$ teaspoon baking soda

1. Preheat the oven to 325°F. Grease a 9-inch by 5-inch loaf pan with cooking spray and dust with flour.

2. Combine the flour, baking powder, and salt in a medium mixing bowl.

3. Combine the butter and sugar in a large mixing bowl and cream with an electric mixer on medium-high speed until fluffy, about 3 minutes, scraping down the sides of the bowl once or twice as necessary. Beat in the eggs, one at a time, scraping down the sides of the bowl after each addition. Beat in the vanilla.

4. With the mixer on low, add $1/3$ of the flour mixture and mix until incorporated. Add $1/2$ of the milk until incorporated. Repeat with the remaining flour and milk, ending with the flour. After the last addition, mix for 30 seconds on medium speed.

5. In a medium mixing bowl, combine the pecans, molasses, corn syrup, and baking soda. Stir $1/3$ of the cake batter into the pecan mixture until well combined.

6. Scrape $1/2$ of the plain batter into the prepared loaf pan and smooth the top. Scrape the molasses batter on top of the plain batter and smooth. Top with the remaining plain batter and smooth the top. Run a butter knife blade through the batter to create marbling. Do not overmix.

7. Bake the pound cake until it is golden brown and a toothpick inserted in the center comes out clean, about 1 hour. Let the cake cool in the pan for about 5 minutes, invert it onto a wire rack, and then turn it right side up on a rack to cool completely. Slice and serve.

8. Store uneaten cake in a cake keeper or wrap in plastic and store at room temperature for up to 3 days.

4 large egg yolks

2/3 cup milk

2 teaspoons pure vanilla extract

2 cups cake flour

1 tablespoon baking powder

1/4 teaspoon salt

1/2 cup (1 stick) unsalted butter, softened

1 1/4 cups sugar

Rich Yellow Loaf Cake

LIGHTER IN TEXTURE than traditional pound cake, this golden loaf is still wonderfully rich tasting because it is made with egg yolks.

1. Preheat the oven to 325°F. Grease a 9-inch by 5-inch loaf pan and dust with flour. Combine the egg yolks, milk, and vanilla in a large glass measuring cup and lightly beat. Combine the flour, baking powder, and salt in a medium mixing bowl.

2. Combine the butter and sugar in a large mixing bowl and cream with an electric mixer on medium-high speed until fluffy, about 3 minutes, scraping down the sides of the bowl once or twice as necessary.

3. With the mixer on medium-low speed, pour the egg mixture into the bowl in a slow stream, stopping the mixer once or twice to scrape down the sides.

4. Turn the mixer to low speed and add the flour mixture, 1/2 cup at a time, scraping down the sides of the bowl after each addition. After the last addition, mix for 1 minute on medium speed.

5. Scrape the batter into the prepared pan and smooth the top with a rubber spatula. Bake the cake until it is golden and a toothpick inserted in the center comes out clean, about 1 hour and 10 minutes. Let the cake cool in the pan for about 5 minutes, invert it onto a wire rack, and then turn it right side up on a rack to cool completely. Slice and serve.

6. Store uneaten cake in a cake keeper or wrap in plastic and store at room temperature for up to 3 days.

Loaf Cake French Toast

USE LEFTOVER SLICES of Rich Yellow Loaf Cake or any other loaf cake to make a decadent breakfast treat. For four 1/2-inch slices of cake, whisk together an egg and 1/2 cup of milk. Dip each slice in the mixture, turning to coat. Melt a tablespoon or so of butter in a nonstick skillet and cook the slices, turning once, until golden and crisp. Rich Yellow Loaf Cake, cooked this way, is great with strawberries and whipped cream. Here are some suggestions for garnishing other types of loaf cake French toast:

ANISE POUND CAKE:
Sweetened sour cream and fig jam

LAVENDER AND LEMON POUND CAKE:
Blueberries and mascarpone

PEANUT BUTTER–CHOCOLATE CHIP POUND CAKE:

Whipped cream and Hershey's® syrup

WALNUT-WHISKEY POUND CAKE:
Maple syrup, of course

TRIPLE GINGER POUND CAKE:
Lemon curd and raspberries

Sweet Potato Pound Cake

BAKED SWEET POTATO is a nice alternative to pumpkin when you want a colorful fall cake. Roasting the potato brings out its flavor and evaporates excess moisture that might make the cake soggy. Whipped cream sweetened with maple syrup would go well here.

1. Preheat the oven to 350°F. Bake the sweet potato until soft, about 1 hour. Cool, peel, and purée. Measure out 1 cup of the purée, setting aside any leftovers for another use.

2. Grease the inside of a 9-inch by 5-inch loaf pan and dust with flour. Combine the flour, baking soda, cinnamon, nutmeg, and salt in a medium bowl.

3. Combine the butter and sugar in a large mixing bowl and cream with an electric mixer on medium-high speed until fluffy, about 3 minutes, scraping down the sides of the bowl once or twice as necessary. Beat in the eggs, one at a time, scraping down the sides of the bowl after each addition. Beat in the sour cream and sweet potato purée. Stir in the vanilla.

4. With the mixer on low, add the flour mixture $1/2$ cup at a time, scraping down the sides of the bowl a few times as necessary. After the last addition, mix for 30 seconds on medium speed.

5. Scrape the batter into the prepared pan and smooth the top with a rubber spatula. Bake until the cake is golden brown and a toothpick inserted into the center comes out clean, 50 to 55 minutes. Let the cake cool in the pan for about 10 minutes, invert it onto a wire rack, then turn it right side up on a rack to cool completely. Slice and serve.

6. Store uneaten cake in a cake keeper or loosely wrap in plastic and store at room temperature for up to 3 days.

Serves 8 to 10

- 1 sweet potato (8 ounces)
- 1$1/2$ cups unbleached all-purpose flour
- $1/2$ teaspoon baking soda
- $1/2$ teaspoon ground cinnamon
- $1/4$ teaspoon ground nutmeg
- $1/4$ teaspoon salt
- $1/2$ cup (1 stick) unsalted butter, softened
- 1$1/4$ cups sugar
- 2 large eggs
- $1/2$ cup sour cream
- 1 teaspoon pure vanilla extract

4 large eggs

1 teaspoon pure vanilla extract

1 teaspoon oriental sesame oil

1 1/2 cups unbleached all-purpose flour

1 teaspoon baking powder

1/4 teaspoon salt

3/4 cup (1 1/2 sticks) unsalted butter, softened

1/2 cup well-stirred tahini

1 cup sugar

6 tablespoons sesame seeds

Sesame Seed Pound Cake

THIS CAKE WAS INSPIRED by a can of tahini paste in my refrigerator. With the addition of some sesame seeds (I like the unhulled ones from the natural foods store) and a teaspoon of oriental sesame oil, it has a deep and wonderful flavor. Serve slices of this fragrant cake in the wintertime with some segmented, sugared pink grapefruit.

1. Preheat the oven to 325°F. Butter the inside of a 9-inch by 5-inch loaf pan and dust with flour.

2. Combine the eggs, vanilla, and sesame oil in a glass measuring cup and lightly beat. Combine the flour, baking powder, and salt in a medium bowl.

3. Combine the butter, tahini, and sugar in a large mixing bowl and cream with an electric mixer on medium-high speed until fluffy, about 3 minutes, scraping down the sides of the bowl once or twice as necessary. With the mixer on medium-low speed, pour the egg mixture into the bowl in a slow stream, stopping once or twice to scrape down the sides of the bowl. Turn the mixer to low and add the flour mixture, 1/2 cup at a time, scraping down the sides of the bowl after each addition. After the last addition, mix on medium speed for 1 minute. Stir in the sesame seeds.

4. Scrape the batter into the prepared pan and smooth the top with a rubber spatula. Sprinkle the top with the remaining 2 tablespoons sesame seeds. Bake until the cake is golden brown and a toothpick inserted into the center comes out clean, about 1 hour and 20 minutes, tenting the cake with foil after about 1 hour if it looks like it is browning too quickly. Let the cake cool in the pan for about 10 minutes, invert it onto a wire rack, and then turn it right side up on a rack to cool completely.

5. Store in a cake keeper for up to 3 days or wrap in plastic and refrigerate for up to 1 week.

¾ cup boiling water

1 bag English breakfast tea

2 cups golden raisins

2 cups unbleached all-purpose flour

½ cup packed light brown sugar

1 teaspoon baking powder

¼ teaspoon baking soda

¼ teaspoon salt

4 tablespoons (½ stick) unsalted butter, softened

1½ tablespoons caraway seeds (optional)

⅔ cup buttermilk

1 large egg, lightly beaten

Tea Cake

THIS NOT-TOO-SWEET LOAF CAKE gets its lovely fragrance from tea-steeped raisins. The caraway seeds, which are optional, make it reminiscent of Irish soda bread. Cool it slightly and serve it warm from the oven if you don't mind your slices a little bit crumbly, or toast slices and spread with jam or clotted cream and serve in the afternoon with tea, of course.

1. Pour the boiling water over the tea bag and let it steep for 5 minutes. Remove the tea bag. Place the raisins in a bowl and pour the hot tea over them. Cover the bowl with plastic wrap and let it stand until the raisins have plumped and cooled to room temperature, about 30 minutes. Drain the raisins, discarding the liquid, and set aside.

2. Preheat the oven to 350°F. Grease the inside of a 9-inch by 5-inch loaf pan and dust with flour.

3. Combine the flour, sugar, baking powder, baking soda, and salt in a large mixing bowl. Add the butter and mix on low speed until the mixture resembles coarse meal. Stir in the plumped raisins and caraway seeds, if using. Stir in the buttermilk and egg and mix smooth.

4. Scrape the batter into the prepared pan and smooth the top with a rubber spatula. Bake until the cake is golden brown and a toothpick inserted into the center comes out clean, about 1 hour. Let the cake cool in the pan for about 5 minutes, invert it onto a wire rack, and then turn it right side up on a rack to cool completely. Slice and serve.

5. Store uneaten cake in a cake keeper or wrap in plastic and store at room temperature for up to 2 days.

Triple Ginger Pound Cake

Serves 8 to 10

THIS POUND CAKE GETS its incredible fragrance from an abundance of ginger, in three forms. In the summer, I serve it with sliced peaches; in the winter, with juicy diced mangoes. Be sure to chop the crystallized ginger finely, so it stays suspended in the batter instead of sinking to the bottom of the pan.

4 large eggs, at room temperature, lightly beaten

1 teaspoon pure vanilla extract

1½ cups cake flour

1 teaspoon ground ginger

¾ teaspoon baking powder

¼ teaspoon salt

1 cup (2 sticks) unsalted butter, softened

1¼ cups sugar

1½ tablespoons grated fresh ginger

½ cup finely chopped crystallized ginger

1. Preheat the oven to 325°F. Grease a 9-inch by 5-inch loaf pan and dust with flour.

2. Combine the eggs and vanilla in a glass measuring cup and lightly beat. Combine the flour, ground ginger, baking powder, and salt in a medium mixing bowl.

3. Combine the butter and sugar in a large mixing bowl and cream with an electric mixer on medium-high speed until fluffy, about 3 minutes, scraping down the sides of the bowl once or twice as necessary.

4. With the mixer on medium-low speed, pour the egg mixture into the bowl in a slow stream, stopping the mixer once or twice to scrape down the sides.

5. Turn the mixer to low speed and add the flour mixture, ½ cup at a time, scraping down the sides of the bowl after each addition. Add the grated ginger and crystallized ginger and mix on medium speed for 30 seconds.

6. Scrape the batter into the prepared pan and smooth the top with a rubber spatula. Bake the cake until it is golden and a toothpick inserted in the center comes out clean, about 1 hour and 15 minutes. Let the cake cool in the pan for about 5 minutes, invert it onto a wire rack, then turn it right side up on a rack to cool completely. Slice and serve.

7. Store uneaten cake in a cake keeper or wrap in plastic and store at room temperature for up to 3 days.

FOR THE CAKE

¼ cup sour cream

¼ cup whiskey

3 large eggs

1 teaspoon pure vanilla extract

1½ cups cake flour

¾ teaspoon baking powder

¼ teaspoon salt

½ cup (1 stick) unsalted butter, softened

1¼ cups packed light brown sugar

½ cup finely chopped walnuts

FOR THE GLAZE

1⅓ cup confectioners' sugar

¼ cup whiskey plus more if necessary

Walnut-Whiskey Pound Cake
with Whiskey Glaze

YOU CAN DEFINITELY TASTE the whiskey in this rustic but grown-up cake, especially when it is drizzled with a potent glaze to match.

MAKE THE CAKE

1. Preheat the oven to 325°F. Grease a 9-inch by 5-inch loaf pan and dust with flour.

2. Combine the sour cream, whiskey, eggs, and vanilla in a large glass measuring cup and lightly beat. Combine the flour, baking powder, and salt in a medium mixing bowl.

3. Combine the butter and brown sugar in a large mixing bowl and cream with an electric mixer on medium-high speed until fluffy, about 3 minutes, scraping down the sides of the bowl once or twice as necessary.

4. With the mixer on medium-low speed, pour the egg mixture into the bowl in a slow stream, stopping the mixer once or twice to scrape down the sides.

5. Turn the mixer to low speed and add the flour mixture, ½ cup at a time, scraping down the sides of the bowl after each addition. After the last addition, mix for 30 seconds on medium speed. Stir in the nuts.

6. Scrape the batter into the prepared pan and smooth the top with a rubber spatula. Bake the cake until it is golden and a toothpick inserted in the center comes out clean, about 1 hour and 15 minutes. Let the cake cool in the pan for about 5 minutes, invert it onto a wire rack, then turn it right side up on a rack to cool completely.

MAKE THE GLAZE

1. Whisk the confectioners' sugar and whiskey together until smooth and pourable. Drizzle the glaze over the top of the cake and some down the sides. Let stand until the glaze hardens, about 30 minutes. Slice and serve.

2. Store uneaten cake in a cake keeper or wrap in plastic and store at room temperature for up to 3 days.

Pumpkin—Chocolate Chip Pound Cake

HERE IS A FAVORITE Halloween treat, combining two seasonal favorites—pumpkin and chocolate—into one delectable pound cake.

1. Preheat the oven to 350°F. Coat the inside of a 9-inch by 5-inch loaf pan with nonstick cooking spray and dust it with flour.

2. Combine the flour, baking soda, baking powder, cinnamon, salt, cloves, and nutmeg in a medium mixing bowl.

3. Combine the butter and sugar in a large mixing bowl and cream with an electric mixer on medium-high speed until fluffy, about 3 minutes, scraping down the sides of the bowl once or twice as necessary.

4. With the mixer on medium-low speed, add the eggs, one at a time, scraping down the sides of the bowl after each addition. Stir in the pumpkin purée and vanilla. Stir in the milk.

5. Turn the mixer to low speed and add the flour mixture, 1/2 cup at a time, scraping down the sides of the bowl after each addition. Stir in the chocolate chips and walnuts.

6. Scrape the batter into the prepared pan and smooth the top with a rubber spatula. Bake the cake until it is firm to the touch and a toothpick inserted in the center comes out clean, 55 minutes to 1 hour. Let the cake cool in the pan for 5 minutes, invert it onto a wire rack, and then turn it right side up on a rack to cool completely.

7. Store uneaten cake in a cake keeper at room temperature for up to 3 days or in the refrigerator, wrapped in plastic, for up to 1 week.

Serves 8

- 1 3/4 cups unbleached all-purpose flour
- 1 teaspoon baking soda
- 1 teaspoon baking powder
- 1 teaspoon ground cinnamon
- 1/2 teaspoon salt
- 1/4 teaspoon ground cloves
- Pinch nutmeg
- 1/2 cup (1 stick) unsalted butter, softened
- 1 1/4 cups sugar
- 3 large eggs
- 1 cup canned pumpkin purée
- 1 teaspoon pure vanilla extract
- 1/3 cup milk
- 1 cup miniature semisweet chocolate chips
- 1 cup chopped walnuts

CHAPTER 4

Bundt Cakes

Hungarian Coffee Cake— recipe on page 119

The Bundt pan, invented in 1950 by H. David Dalquist, the founder of Nordic Ware®, is the world's best-selling cake pan, with more than 50 million sold worldwide, which may be why it merits its own holiday—November 15 is National Bundt Pan Day. Even if you haven't baked a Bundt cake in recent memory, chances are you have a pan languishing in a kitchen cabinet. There are several reasons why Bundt cakes are so popular:

- While cakes baked in round or square pans can dry out around the edges before the center is done, cakes baked in a tubular pan bake evenly and relatively quickly.

- Bundt pans hold roughly twice the volume of round or square pans, yet the average Bundt cake takes only a few minutes longer to bake than the smaller cakes.

- The pan's folds produce a beautifully sculpted cake, so there's no need for fancy frosting and decorating.

- Not only is the dramatic shape of a Bundt cake attractive, but it also provides a guide for even slicing of the cake.

Since its introduction so many years ago, the Bundt pan has been redesigned numerous times, so you can now make a Bundt cake in the shape of rose, a Star of David, or a stand of evergreen trees. With these more complicated molds, and their deeper folds, comes a greater risk of the cake sticking to the inside of the pan. Even if treated with a nonstick coating, a pan may grab and hold a portion of your cake as you attempt to unmold it. To win this battle, be sure to grease your pan well, brushing vegetable shortening into every nook and cranny, and flour the pan, to boot. Or try a grease-and-flour spray like Baker's Joy, which combines the two steps and guarantees good coverage of even the most intricately patterned pans.

FOR THE STREUSEL

1 cup firmly packed brown sugar

1 cup rolled oats (not quick-cooking)

1 tablespoon ground cinnamon

6 tablespoons (³/₄ stick) unsalted butter, cut into bits and chilled

FOR THE CAKE

2¹/₂ cups unbleached all-purpose flour

1¹/₂ cups granulated sugar

2¹/₂ teaspoons baking powder

1 teaspoon ground cardamom

¹/₂ teaspoon ground cloves

1 teaspoon salt

2 cups unsweetened applesauce

2 large eggs, lightly beaten

¹/₂ cup (1 stick) unsalted butter, melted

1 teaspoon pure vanilla extract

¹/₂ cup vegetable oil

Applesauce Cake
with Oatmeal Streusel

BUTTER ADDS GREAT RICHNESS to this spicy streusel cake, while oil and applesauce make it wonderfully moist. The flavor of the applesauce really comes forward after a day or two, making this a great cake for keeping and snacking.

MAKE THE STREUSEL

1. Combine the brown sugar, oats, and cinnamon in a medium bowl. Add the butter and work it into the other ingredients with your fingers until it is crumbly, with no pieces larger than small peas. Refrigerate until needed.

MAKE THE CAKE

1. Preheat the oven to 350°F. Grease a 12-cup Bundt pan and dust with flour.

2. Whisk together the flour, granulated sugar, baking powder, cardamom, cloves, and salt in a large mixing bowl. Whisk in the applesauce, eggs, butter, vanilla, and vegetable oil.

3. Scrape ¹/₂ of the batter into the prepared pan. Sprinkle ¹/₂ of the streusel over the batter. Repeat with the remaining batter and streusel. Bake until a toothpick inserted into the center comes out clean, about 1 hour and 15 minutes. Let the cake cool in the pan for about 10 minutes, then invert it onto a wire rack to cool completely. Slice and serve.

4. Store uneaten cake in a cake keeper or wrap in plastic and store at room temperature for up to 5 days.

Banana–Chocolate Chip Bundt Cake

THIS IS A CLASSIC, LONG-KEEPING Bundt cake that I couldn't live without. Make sure your bananas are very ripe (brown all over) for the best banana flavor.

1. Preheat the oven to 375°F. Grease a 12-cup Bundt pan and dust with flour.

2. Whisk together the eggs, bananas, sour cream, and vanilla in a large glass measuring cup. Whisk together the flour, baking powder, baking soda, and salt in a medium bowl.

3. Combine the butter and sugar in a large mixing bowl and cream with an electric mixer on medium-high speed until fluffy, about 3 minutes, scraping down the sides of the bowl once or twice as necessary.

4. With the mixer on medium-low speed, pour the sour cream mixture into the bowl in a slow stream, stopping the mixer once or twice to scrape down the bowl. With the mixer on low speed, add the flour mixture a little at a time, scraping down the sides of the bowl after each addition and beating until smooth. Stir in the walnuts and chocolate chips.

5. Pour the batter into the prepared pan. Bake until a toothpick inserted in the center comes out clean, about 45 minutes. Let the cake cool in the pan for 5 minutes, then invert it onto a wire rack to cool completely. Dust with cocoa powder and serve.

6. Store uneaten cake in a cake keeper or wrap in plastic and store at room temperature for up to 5 days.

Serves 10 to 12

2 large eggs

3 very ripe medium-size bananas, mashed (about 1¼ cups)

⅔ cup sour cream

1 teaspoon pure vanilla extract

2¼ cups unbleached all-purpose flour

1 teaspoon baking powder

½ teaspoon baking soda

½ teaspoon salt

½ cup (1 stick) unsalted butter, softened

1 cup sugar

1 cup walnuts, coarsely chopped

1 cup bittersweet or semisweet chocolate chips

Cocoa powder for dusting

FOR THE CAKE

1¼ cups buttermilk

3 large eggs, room temperature

1 teaspoon pure vanilla extract

2 cups unbleached all-purpose flour

1 cup walnuts, toasted, cooled, and finely chopped

1 teaspoon baking powder

1 teaspoon baking soda

½ teaspoon salt

2 teaspoons ground cinnamon

1 teaspoon ground cardamom

½ teaspoon ground cloves

1 teaspoon ground black pepper

1 cup (2 sticks) unsalted butter, softened

1 cup sugar

FOR THE GLAZE

1 cup confectioners' sugar

2 tablespoons fresh lemon juice

Black Pepper and Spice Cake with Lemon Glaze

I LOVE SPICE CAKES, and this one in particular, with its combination of cinnamon, cardamom, cloves, and ground black pepper. The lemon glaze contrasts wonderfully with the peppery cake.

MAKE THE CAKE

1. Preheat the oven to 350°F. Grease a 12-cup Bundt pan and dust with flour.

2. Whisk together the buttermilk, eggs, and vanilla in a large glass measuring cup. Whisk together the flour, nuts, baking powder, baking soda, salt, cinnamon, cardamom, cloves, and black pepper in a medium bowl.

3. Combine the butter and sugar in a large mixing bowl and cream with an electric mixer on medium-high speed until fluffy, about 3 minutes, scraping down the sides of the bowl once or twice as necessary.

4. With the mixer on low speed, add ⅓ of the flour mixture and beat until incorporated. Add ½ of the buttermilk mixture. Repeat, alternating flour and buttermilk mixtures and ending with the flour mixture, scraping down the sides of the bowl between additions. Turn the mixer to medium-high speed and beat for 1 minute.

5. Scrape the batter into the prepared pan. Bake until a toothpick inserted in the center comes out clean, 40 to 45 minutes. Let the cake cool in the pan for 5 minutes, then invert it onto a wire rack to cool completely.

MAKE THE GLAZE

1. Whisk together the confectioners' sugar and lemon juice in a medium bowl until smooth. Drizzle over the cake, letting it drip down the sides. Let stand until the glaze is set, about ½ hour. Slice and serve.

2. Store uneaten cake in a cake keeper or wrap in plastic and store at room temperature for up to 3 days.

- ½ cup unsweetened Dutch process cocoa powder plus more for dusting the pan
- ½ cup sour cream
- 3 large eggs
- 2 teaspoons pure vanilla extract
- 2½ cups unbleached all-purpose flour
- 2½ teaspoons baking powder
- 1½ teaspoons baking soda
- 1 teaspoon salt
- 2 teaspoons instant espresso powder
- ¾ cup (1½ sticks) butter, softened
- 1 cup granulated sugar
- 1 cup packed light brown sugar
- 2 cups coarsely shredded zucchini
- 1 cup semisweet chocolate chips
- 1 cup sliced almonds

Chocolate-Zucchini Bundt Cake

TURN TO THIS RECIPE when you desperately need a new way to use some of your bumper crop of zucchini. It gives this not-too-sweet chocolate cake terrific moisture and a mysterious but delicious vegetal flavor. The sliced almonds provide some crunch.

1. Preheat the oven to 350°F. Grease a 12-cup Bundt pan and dust with unsweetened cocoa powder.

2. Whisk together the sour cream, eggs, and vanilla in a large glass measuring cup. Whisk together the flour, ½ cup cocoa powder, baking powder, baking soda, salt, and espresso powder in a medium bowl.

3. Combine the butter and sugars in a large mixing bowl and cream with an electric mixer on medium-high speed until fluffy, about 3 minutes, scraping down the sides of the bowl once or twice as necessary.

4. With the mixer on low speed, add ⅓ of the flour mixture and beat until incorporated. Add ½ of the sour cream mixture. Repeat, alternating flour and sour cream mixtures and ending with the flour mixture, scraping down the sides of the bowl between additions. Stir in the zucchini, chocolate chips, and nuts.

5. Scrape the batter into the prepared pan. Bake until a toothpick inserted in the center comes out clean, 45 to 50 minutes. Let cool in the pan for 10 minutes, then invert it onto a wire rack to cool completely. Slice and serve.

6. Store uneaten cake in a cake keeper or wrap in plastic and store at room temperature for up to 3 days.

Dulce de Leche Coffee Cake

Serves 8 to 10

- 1 1/4 cups coarsely chopped walnuts
- 1 cup semisweet chocolate chips
- 1 tablespoon ground cinnamon
- 1 1/4 cups dulce de leche
- 3 large eggs
- 1 cup sour cream
- 1 tablespoon vanilla extract
- 2 3/4 cups unbleached all-purpose flour
- 1/2 teaspoon baking soda
- 1 1/2 teaspoons baking powder
- 1/2 teaspoon salt
- 3/4 cup (1 1/2 sticks) unsalted butter, room temperature
- 1 1/2 cups sugar

DULCE DE LECHE, a Mexican-style caramel sauce available in specialty grocery stores and many supermarkets, gives the streusel in this cake a candy-like gooey chewiness. To dress it up for a party, serve with small scoops of chocolate ice cream and sweetened whipped cream spiced with a little ground cinnamon.

MAKE THE STREUSEL

1. Preheat the oven to 350°F. Coat the inside of a 12-cup Bundt pan with cooking spray and dust it with flour.

2. Combine the nuts, chocolate chips, and cinnamon in a medium bowl. Drizzle the dulce de leche over the mixture and toss with a spoon to coat. Set aside.

MAKE THE CAKE

1. Combine the eggs, sour cream, and vanilla in a large glass measuring cup and lightly beat. Combine the flour, baking soda, baking powder, and salt in a medium mixing bowl.

2. Combine the butter and sugar in a large mixing bowl and cream with an electric mixer on medium-high speed until fluffy, about 3 minutes, scraping down the sides of the bowl once or twice as necessary.

3. With the mixer on medium-low speed, pour 1/3 of the egg mixture into the bowl in a slow stream. Add 1/3 of the flour mixture. Add another 1/3 of the egg mixture and another 1/3 of the flour mixture. Add the remaining egg mixture and then the remaining flour mixture. Scrape down the sides of the bowl and beat on medium speed for 1 minute.

4. Scrape 1/3 of the batter into the prepared pan. Sprinkle with 1/3 of the dulce de leche mixture. Repeat two more times. Bake the cake until it is golden and a toothpick inserted in the center comes out clean, 55 minutes to 1 hour. Let the cake cool in the pan for 15 minutes, then invert it onto a wire rack to cool completely. Slice and serve.

5. Store uneaten cake in a cake keeper or wrap in plastic and store at room temperature for up to 3 days.

2 cups unbleached all-purpose flour

1 cup yellow cornmeal

2 teaspoons baking powder

1 teaspoon baking soda

$\frac{1}{2}$ teaspoon salt

$2\frac{1}{4}$ cups packed light brown sugar

1 cup (2 sticks) unsalted butter, softened

3 large eggs

2 teaspoons pure vanilla extract

$\frac{3}{4}$ cup buttermilk

1 pint blueberries, washed and picked over

Blueberry-Cornmeal Bundt Cake

CORNMEAL GIVES THIS CAKE a lovely sandy texture and a nice crunchy crust. Brown sugar gives it a hint of molasses flavor, which is a good match with the blueberries. Fresh blueberries are great, but, in the winter when they're scarce and costly, you can substitute frozen. Use frozen berries straight from the freezer, and add 5 to 10 minutes of baking time to the cake, since they will cool the batter down once they're stirred in.

For everyday eating, this cake needs no embellishment. For a dinner party, slices may be dressed up with molasses whipped cream: Whip 1 cup of heavy cream with 1 tablespoon of confectioners' sugar, then gently fold in 1 tablespoon of dark molasses, without overmixing, so some streaks of molasses are visible in the whipped cream.

1. Preheat the oven to 350°F. Grease a 12-cup Bundt pan and dust with flour.

2. Whisk together the flour, cornmeal, baking powder, baking soda, and salt in a medium bowl.

3. Combine the brown sugar and butter in a large bowl and beat with an electric mixer until fluffy, about 3 minutes, scraping down the sides of the bowl as necessary. Add the eggs and beat, scraping down the bowl once or twice, until smooth. Stir in the vanilla. Stir in the flour mixture in 3 additions, alternating with the buttermilk in 2 additions, and ending with the flour. Stir in the blueberries.

4. Scrape the batter into the prepared pan and smooth the top with a rubber spatula. Bake until the cake is golden and a toothpick inserted in the center comes out clean, 1 hour to 1 hour and 15 minutes. Let the cake cool in the pan for 10 minutes, invert it onto a wire rack, and cool completely. Slice and serve.

5. Store uneaten cake in a cake keeper or wrap in plastic and store at room temperature for up to 3 days.

3 eggs

¾ cup sour cream

1 teaspoon pure vanilla extract

1½ cups unbleached all-purpose flour

½ cup unsweetened Dutch process cocoa powder

2 teaspoons baking powder

½ teaspoon baking soda

¼ teaspoon salt

¾ cup (1½ sticks) unsalted butter, softened

1 cup packed light brown sugar

1 cup granulated sugar

1 cup prunes, chopped

1 cup walnuts, toasted and coarsely chopped

⅓ cup Armagnac or brandy

Chocolate, Walnut, and Prune Cake

THIS BROWNIE-LIKE CAKE is moist and dark, studded with chopped prunes and walnuts and flavored with Armagnac. Vanilla ice cream finishes it off nicely for a party.

1. Preheat the oven to 325°F. Grease a 12-cup Bundt pan and dust with flour.

2. Combine the eggs, sour cream, and vanilla in a glass measuring cup and lightly beat. Combine the flour, cocoa powder, baking powder, baking soda, and salt in a medium mixing bowl.

3. Combine the butter and sugars in a large mixing bowl and cream with an electric mixer on medium-high speed until fluffy, about 3 minutes, scraping down the sides of the bowl once or twice as necessary.

4. With the mixer on medium-low speed, pour the egg mixture into the bowl in a slow stream, stopping the mixer once or twice to scrape down the sides.

5. Turn the mixer on low speed and add the flour mixture, ½ cup at a time, scraping down the sides of the bowl after each addition. Mix in the prunes, walnuts, and Armagnac until just combined. Do not overmix.

6. Scrape the batter into the prepared pan and smooth the top with a rubber spatula. Bake the cake until it is firm and a toothpick inserted in the center comes out clean, about 1 hour and 10 minutes. Let the cake cool in the pan for about 5 minutes, then invert it onto a wire rack to cool completely. Slice and serve.

7. Store uneaten cake in a cake keeper or wrap in plastic and store at room temperature for up to 5 days.

3 cups cake flour

1½ teaspoons baking powder

1 teaspoon salt

1 cup (2 sticks) unsalted butter, softened

8 ounces cream cheese, softened

2½ cups sugar

6 eggs, room temperature

1 tablespoon pure vanilla extract

1½ tablespoons grated fresh ginger

1 tablespoon grated lemon zest

Cold-Oven Cream Cheese Pound Cake

BAKING THIS POUND CAKE in a cold oven gives it time to rise to great heights while developing a beautiful golden-brown crust. The cream cheese gives it an unbelievably velvety crumb.

1. Adjust the oven rack to the lower-middle position. Grease a 12-cup Bundt pan and dust with flour. Combine the flour, baking powder, and salt in a medium mixing bowl.

2. Combine the butter, cream cheese, and sugar in a large mixing bowl and cream with an electric mixer on medium-high speed until fluffy, about 3 minutes, scraping down the sides of the bowl as necessary.

3. With the mixer on medium speed, add the eggs, one at a time, scraping down the sides of the bowl after each addition. Beat in the vanilla, ginger, and lemon zest.

4. Turn the mixer to low speed and add the flour mixture, ½ cup at a time, scraping down the sides of the bowl after each addition. After the last addition, mix for 30 seconds on medium speed.

5. Place the cake in a cold oven. Turn the oven to 325°F and bake, without opening the oven door, until the cake is golden brown and a toothpick inserted in the center comes out clean, 65 to 80 minutes.

6. Cool the cake in pan for 15 minutes, then invert it onto rack. Cool completely before slicing and serving.

7. Store uneaten cake in a cake keeper or wrap in plastic and store at room temperature for up to 3 days.

Cream Cake

HERE'S AN INTRIGUINGLY SIMPLE recipe for a plain yellow Bundt cake, rich in eggs and heavy cream but with no butter. Instead of adding air to the batter by creaming, you whip the eggs and sugar together to pump it up, then just beat in the cream and dry ingredients. It bakes up big and beautiful, light and tender, and not at all greasy, great for keeping around for after-school snacking. Or serve it at a big party with some juicy fruit or berries to add color and flavor.

1. Preheat the oven to 350°F. Grease a 12-cup Bundt pan and dust with flour. Combine the flour, baking powder, and salt in a medium mixing bowl.

2. Combine the eggs and sugar in a large mixing bowl. Beat on medium-high speed until the mixture is pale yellow and thickened, about 5 minutes. Stir in the vanilla.

3. With the mixer on medium-low speed, pour $1/3$ of the cream into the bowl in a slow stream. Add $1/3$ of the flour mixture. Add another $1/3$ of the cream and another $1/3$ of the flour mixture. Add the remaining cream, then the remaining flour mixture. Scrape down the sides of the bowl and beat on medium speed for 1 minute.

4. Scrape the batter into the prepared pan. Bake the cake until it is golden brown and a toothpick inserted in the center comes out clean, about 1 hour. Check on it after 45 minutes, and if the top is already brown, loosely tent it with foil. Let the cake cool in the pan for 15 minutes, then invert onto a wire rack to cool completely. Slice and serve.

5. Store uneaten cake in a cake keeper or wrap in plastic and store at room temperature for up to 3 days.

Serves 12 to 16

3 cups unbleached all-purpose flour

1 tablespoon baking powder

$1/2$ teaspoon salt

6 large eggs, room temperature

$2^3/4$ cups sugar

1 tablespoon pure vanilla extract

2 cups heavy cream, room temperature

FOR THE STREUSEL

½ cup firmly packed light brown sugar

1 cup walnuts, toasted and coarsely chopped

2 teaspoons instant espresso powder

FOR THE CAKE

4 large eggs

1 cup sour cream (not lowfat or nonfat)

2 teaspoons pure vanilla extract

1 teaspoon maple extract

3 cups unbleached all-purpose flour

1 teaspoon baking soda

2 teaspoons baking powder

½ teaspoon salt

1 cup (2 sticks) unsalted butter, softened

1½ cups packed light brown sugar

2 cups dried cranberries

FOR THE GLAZE

1 cup confectioners' sugar

2 tablespoons pure maple syrup

3 tablespoons heavy cream

2 teaspoons instant espresso powder

Cranberry-Walnut Bundt Cake with Maple-Espresso Glaze

COFFEE IS A SURPRISING but terrific flavor match for tart cranberries and sweet maple in this Bundt cake. It's a real fall treat, especially when served with coffee ice cream.

MAKE THE STREUSEL

1. Preheat the oven to 325°F. Grease a 12-cup Bundt pan and dust with flour.

2. Combine the brown sugar, walnuts, and espresso powder in a bowl and set aside.

MAKE THE CAKE

1. Combine the eggs, sour cream, vanilla, and maple extract in a measuring cup and lightly beat. Combine the flour, baking soda, baking powder, and salt in a bowl.

2. Combine the butter and brown sugar in a large mixing bowl and cream with an electric mixer on medium-high speed until fluffy, about 3 minutes, scraping down the sides of the bowl once or twice as necessary.

3. With the mixer on medium-low, pour ⅓ of the egg mixture into the bowl in a slow stream. Add ⅓ of the flour mixture. Add another ⅓ of the egg mixture and another ⅓ of the flour mixture. Add the remaining egg mixture, then the remaining flour mixture. Scrape down the sides of the bowl and beat on medium speed for 1 minute. Stir in the cranberries.

4. Scrape ⅓ of the batter into the pan. Sprinkle with ⅓ of the walnut mixture. Repeat twice. Bake until a toothpick comes out clean, 1 hour to 1 hour and 10 minutes. Let the cake cool for 15 minutes, then invert onto a wire rack to cool.

MAKE THE GLAZE

1. Whisk together the confectioners' sugar, maple syrup, cream, and espresso powder in a medium bowl. Place the cake on a wire rack set over a baking sheet. Slowly drizzle the glaze over the cake, allowing it to run down the sides of the cake, covering as much of the cake as possible. Spoon any glaze drippings from the baking sheet over the cake. Let the glaze set for 30 minutes. Slice and serve. Store uneaten cake in a cake keeper or wrap in plastic and store at room temperature for up to 5 days.

FOR THE CAKE

$2/3$ cup sour cream

4 large eggs

1 teaspoon vanilla extract

1 cup hazelnuts, toasted, skinned, and finely chopped

1 tablespoon instant espresso powder

$1\frac{1}{3}$ cups unbleached all-purpose flour

2 teaspoons baking powder

$\frac{1}{4}$ teaspoon baking soda

$\frac{1}{4}$ teaspoon salt

10 tablespoons ($1\frac{1}{4}$ sticks) unsalted butter, softened

1 cup sugar

FOR THE GLAZE

8 ounces bittersweet or semisweet chocolate, finely chopped

2 tablespoons vegetable oil

1 tablespoon light corn syrup

$\frac{1}{4}$ teaspoon pure vanilla extract

Espresso-Hazelnut Bundt Cake

THE COMBINATION OF COFFEE and hazelnuts isn't a hard sell, especially when it comes in the form of a beautiful Bundt cake with a shiny chocolate glaze.

MAKE THE CAKE

1. Preheat the oven to 350°F. Grease a 12-cup Bundt pan and dust with flour. Whisk together the sour cream, eggs, and vanilla in a large glass measuring cup. Whisk together the nuts, espresso powder, flour, baking powder, baking soda, and salt in a medium bowl.

2. Combine the butter and sugar in a large bowl and cream with an electric mixer on medium-high speed until fluffy, scraping down the sides of the bowl as necessary.

3. With the mixer on low speed, add $1/3$ of the flour mixture and beat until incorporated. Add $1/2$ of the sour cream mixture. Repeat, alternating flour and sour cream mixtures and ending with the flour mixture, scraping down the sides of the bowl between additions. Turn the mixer to medium-high speed and beat for 1 minute.

4. Scrape the batter into the prepared pan. Bake until a toothpick inserted in the center comes out clean, 35 to 40 minutes. Let cool in the pan for 5 minutes, then invert it onto a wire rack to cool completely.

MAKE THE GLAZE

1. Put 1 inch of water in the bottom of a double boiler or medium saucepan and bring to a bare simmer. Combine the chocolate, oil, and corn syrup in the top of the double boiler or in a stainless steel bowl and set it on top of the simmering water, making sure that the water doesn't touch the bottom of the bowl. Heat, whisking occasionally, until the chocolate is completely melted. Stir in the vanilla. Drizzle over the cake, letting it drip down the sides. Let stand until the glaze is set, about 1 hour. Slice and serve.

2. Store uneaten cake in a cake keeper or wrap in plastic and store at room temperature for up to 3 days.

Hungarian Coffee Cake

THIS PULL-APART COFFEE CAKE (also known as Monkey Bread, but somehow that name just isn't as appetizing) will surely test your self-control if you are a fan of cinnamon buns. The cake is made by coating individual balls of buttermilk biscuit dough in cinnamon sugar, layering them in a Bundt pan with nuts and raisins, and then pouring a caramel topping made of melted butter and brown sugar over the assembled cake just before baking. Do use a nonstick pan, because the caramel is quite sticky. Make sure you cool the butter before you combine it with the brown sugar and pour it over the cake, so the biscuits stay nice and cool until they hit the oven.

MAKE THE TOPPING

1. Whisk together the melted butter and light brown sugar. Set aside.

MAKE THE CAKE

1. Preheat the oven to 350°F. Grease a nonstick 12-cup Bundt pan and dust with flour.

2. Combine the granulated sugar and cinnamon in a zipper-top bag. Cut the butter into ¼-inch dice. Place the butter in a small bowl and set it in the freezer while you gather together the rest of the cake ingredients.

3. Combine the flour, baking powder, baking soda, and salt in a large mixing bowl. Add the chilled butter pieces and, with an electric mixer, mix on low speed until the mixture resembles coarse meal. Stir in the buttermilk until the mixture just comes together, adding an extra tablespoon or two if the mixture is too dry.

4. Use a small ice cream scoop or spoon to scoop up balls of dough and transfer them to the zipper-top bag. Shake the bag to coat the balls with cinnamon sugar.

5. Place the coated balls of dough in the prepared pan, sprinkling walnuts and raisins over them as you go. Pour the melted butter mixture over the cake. Bake until the cake is firm and well risen and the caramel is melted, 35 to 40 minutes. Let the cake cool in the pan, on a wire rack, for 10 minutes. Invert onto a serving platter and serve immediately.

6. Store uneaten cake in a cake keeper or wrap in plastic and store at room temperature for up to 1 day.

Serves 10 to 12

FOR THE TOPPING

½ cup (1 stick) unsalted butter, melted and cooled

¾ cup light brown sugar

FOR THE CAKE

½ cup granulated sugar

1 teaspoon ground cinnamon

9 tablespoons unsalted butter, chilled

3 cups unbleached all-purpose flour

1 tablespoon baking powder

¾ teaspoon baking soda

¾ teaspoon salt

1 cup plus 2 tablespoons buttermilk, plus more if necessary

¼ cup walnuts, chopped

¼ cup raisins

FOR THE CAKE

2 cups unbleached all-purpose flour

2 teaspoons baking soda

2 teaspoons instant espresso powder

$1/2$ teaspoon salt

1 cup (2 sticks) unsalted butter, cut into pieces

6 ounces unsweetened chocolate, finely chopped

$1/2$ cup brewed espresso

$1 1/2$ cups granulated sugar

$1/2$ cup bourbon

4 large eggs

1 teaspoon pure vanilla extract

$3/4$ cup mini chocolate chips

FOR THE GLAZE

6 tablespoons ($3/4$ stick) unsalted butter, cut into pieces

6 tablespoons packed light brown sugar

2 teaspoons instant espresso powder

6 tablespoons heavy cream

$1 1/2$ cups confectioners' sugar

2 tablespoons bourbon

Mississippi Mud Cake with Espresso-Bourbon Glaze

THIS IS A RECIPE I've been tinkering with for about 10 years now. Lately, I've been adding miniature chocolate chips, which give the cake some added moisture as well as chocolate flavor. You can also add a cup of finely chopped pecans for extra southern goodness.

MAKE THE CAKE

1. Preheat the oven to 350°F. Grease a 12-cup Bundt pan and dust with flour. Combine the flour, baking soda, espresso powder, and salt in a medium mixing bowl.

2. Combine the butter, chocolate, and espresso in a medium saucepan. Heat over medium, stirring, until the butter and chocolate are melted. Remove from the heat and stir in the granulated sugar and bourbon.

3. Place the eggs and vanilla in a large mixing bowl and beat with an electric mixer on low to break up the eggs. Beat in the chocolate mixture. Add the flour mixture and stir until just combined. Stir in the chocolate chips.

4. Scrape the batter into the prepared pan and smooth the top with a spatula. Bake until a toothpick inserted into the center of the cake comes out clean, about 45 minutes. Let the cake cool in the pan for 5 minutes and then invert it onto a wire rack to cool completely.

MAKE THE GLAZE

1. Stir the butter, brown sugar, and espresso powder together in a small saucepan over medium heat until the butter is melted. Whisk in the cream and bring to a simmer. Cook for 1 minute, remove from the heat, and whisk in the confectioners' sugar until smooth. Mix in the bourbon. Let cool for 10 minutes.

2. Place the cake, still on the wire rack, over a baking sheet. Slowly drizzle the glaze over the cake, letting it run down the sides of the cake and covering as much of the cake as possible. Let stand until the glaze is set, about $1/2$ hour. Slice and serve.

3. Store uneaten cake in a cake keeper or wrap in plastic and store at room temperature for up to 3 days.

Triple Chocolate Bundt Cake

UNSWEETENED CHOCOLATE, cocoa powder, and chocolate chips work together to give this cake deep chocolate flavor. Use miniature chocolate chips, which will stay suspended in the batter. Bigger ones may sink to the bottom of the pan.

1. Preheat the oven to 350°F. Grease a 12-cup Bundt pan and dust with flour.

2. Place the chocolate and cocoa powder in a medium heatproof bowl. Pour the boiling water over the chocolate and whisk until smooth. Set aside to cool.

3. Whisk together the milk, eggs, and vanilla in a large glass measuring cup. Whisk together the flour, baking powder, baking soda, and salt.

4. Combine the butter and sugar in a large mixing bowl and cream with an electric mixer on medium-high speed until fluffy, about 3 minutes, scraping down the sides of the bowl once or twice as necessary. Add the chocolate mixture and mix on low until well combined.

5. With the mixer on low speed, add $1/3$ of the flour mixture and beat until incorporated. Add $1/2$ of the milk mixture. Repeat, alternating flour and milk mixtures and ending with the flour mixture, scraping down the sides of the bowl between additions. Turn the mixer to medium-high speed and beat for 1 minute. Stir in the chocolate chips.

6. Scrape the batter into the prepared pan. Bake until a toothpick inserted in the center comes out clean, 50 to 60 minutes. Let the cake cool in the pan for 5 minutes, then invert it onto a wire rack to cool completely. Slice and serve.

7. Store uneaten cake in a cake keeper or wrap in plastic and store at room temperature for up to 3 days.

Serves 10 to 12

4 ounces unsweetened chocolate, finely chopped

$1/3$ cup unsweetened Dutch process cocoa powder

1 cup boiling water

1 cup milk

3 large eggs

1 tablespoon pure vanilla extract

$2 1/4$ cups unbleached all-purpose flour

2 teaspoons baking powder

1 teaspoon baking soda

$1/4$ teaspoon salt

1 cup (2 sticks) unsalted butter, softened

2 cups sugar

$1 1/2$ cups mini chocolate chips

FOR THE CAKE

3 cups unbleached all-purpose flour

1½ teaspoons baking powder

½ teaspoon baking soda

1 teaspoon salt

¾ cup (1½ sticks) unsalted butter, softened

1½ cups sugar

1½ cups whole milk ricotta cheese

3 large eggs

¼ cup orange juice

1½ teaspoons pure vanilla extract

1½ teaspoons orange zest

FOR THE GLAZE

½ cup orange marmalade

2 teaspoons water

Orange-Ricotta Pound Cake
with Marmalade Glaze

RICOTTA CHEESE IS THE DAIRY component here, and it gives this pound cake a moist, light texture. The glaze gives the cake a wonderful shine and keeps it fresh for days. Orange marmalade is easiest to find, but you may substitute grapefruit zest and grapefruit marmalade with great results if you like.

MAKE THE CAKE

1. Preheat the oven to 325°F. Grease a 12-cup Bundt pan and dust with flour. Combine the flour, baking powder, baking soda, and salt in a medium mixing bowl.

2. Combine the butter and sugar in a large mixing bowl and cream with an electric mixer on medium-high speed until fluffy, about 3 minutes, scraping down the sides of the bowl as necessary. Add the ricotta cheese and beat until smooth.

3. With the mixer on medium speed, add the eggs, one at a time, scraping down the sides of the bowl after each addition. Beat in the orange juice, vanilla, and orange zest.

4. Turn the mixer to low speed and add the flour mixture, ½ cup at a time, scraping down the sides of the bowl after each addition. After the last addition, mix for 30 seconds on medium speed.

5. Scrape the batter into the prepared pan. Bake until the cake is golden brown and a toothpick inserted in the center comes out clean, about 1 hour and 10 minutes.

6. Cool the cake in the pan for 15 minutes, then invert it onto a rack to cool completely.

MAKE THE GLAZE

1. Stir the marmalade and water together in a small saucepan over medium heat until the marmalade liquefies. Brush the hot mixture over the cake. Let the glaze cool and set before slicing and serving.

2. Store uneaten cake in a cake keeper or wrap in plastic and store at room temperature for up to 3 days.

¾ cup (1½ sticks) unsalted butter

1 tablespoon finely chopped fresh sage leaves

2½ cups unbleached all-purpose flour

2 teaspoons baking powder

2 teaspoons ground ginger

1 teaspoon salt

1 cup granulated sugar

1 cup packed light brown sugar

1 can (15 ounces) pumpkin purée

3 large eggs

1 teaspoon pure vanilla extract

1 cup chopped walnuts

Pumpkin-Sage Ring

SINCE MAKING MY LAVENDER and Lemon Pound Cake (see page 86), I've been intrigued by the idea of using herbs in simple cakes. Pumpkin and sage are a wonderful savory combination, so I wondered what they would taste like together in a sweet form. I was very pleased with the result—a more interesting and sophisticated pumpkin cake, for sure. Finish off slices with some maple syrup–sweetened crème fraîche.

1. Preheat the oven to 375°F. Grease a 12-cup Bundt pan and dust with flour. Combine the butter and sage in a small pan and heat on low until the butter is melted. Set aside to cool.

2. Whisk together the flour, baking powder, ginger, and salt in a medium mixing bowl. Whisk together the butter and sage mixture, granulated sugar, brown sugar, pumpkin, eggs, and vanilla in a large mixing bowl. Stir the flour into the pumpkin mixture until combined. Stir in the chopped nuts.

3. Scrape the batter into the prepared pan. Bake until a toothpick inserted in the center comes out clean, 40 to 45 minutes. Let cool in the pan for 5 minutes, then invert it onto a wire rack to cool completely. Slice and serve.

4. Store uneaten cake in a cake keeper or wrap in plastic and store at room temperature for up to 3 days.

1½ cups plain whole-milk yogurt or lowfat yogurt

1 cup yellow cornmeal

2 cups unbleached all-purpose flour

2 teaspoons baking powder

1 teaspoon baking soda

1 teaspoon salt

1½ cups shelled unsalted pistachios

¾ cup (1½ sticks) unsalted butter, softened

1½ cups sugar

3 large eggs

1 teaspoon pure vanilla extract

Pistachio-Polenta Pound Cake

SOME OF THE PISTACHIOS in this cake are ground fine, so their flavorful oils moisten the batter. The rest are chopped to give the cake beautiful crunch, also provided by the cornmeal. I love this cake with orange sections tossed with a little sugar and sprinkled with Grand Marnier.®

1. Whisk together the yogurt and cornmeal in a medium bowl and let it stand for 45 minutes.

2. Preheat the oven to 350°F. Grease a 12-cup Bundt pan and dust with flour. Combine the flour, baking powder, baking soda, and salt in a medium mixing bowl.

3. Grind ¾ cup of the pistachios finely in a food processor. Chop the remaining ¾ cup pistachios coarsely and set aside.

4. Combine the butter, sugar, and ground pistachios in a large mixing bowl and cream with an electric mixer on medium-high speed until fluffy, about 3 minutes, scraping down the sides of the bowl as necessary.

5. With the mixer on medium speed, add the eggs, one at a time, scraping down the sides of the bowl after each addition. Beat in the vanilla.

6. With the mixer on low speed, add ⅓ of the flour mixture and beat until incorporated. Add ½ of the yogurt mixture. Repeat, alternating flour and yogurt mixtures and ending with the flour mixture, scraping down the sides of the bowl between additions. Stir in the chopped pistachios.

7. Scrape the batter into the prepared pan. Bake until a toothpick inserted in the center comes out clean, 45 to 50 minutes. Let the cake cool in the pan for 10 minutes, then invert it onto a wire rack to cool completely. Slice and serve.

8. Store uneaten cake in a cake keeper or wrap in plastic and store at room temperature for up to 3 days.

FOR THE CAKE

1 1/2 cups sweetened flaked coconut

2 large eggs

1 cup sour cream

1 teaspoon pure vanilla extract

1 3/4 cups all-purpose flour

1 1/2 teaspoons baking powder

1/4 teaspoon baking soda

1/4 teaspoon salt

1/2 cup (1 stick) unsalted butter, softened

3/4 cup sugar

1 can (20 ounces) pineapple chunks in juice, drained well and patted dry

FOR THE GLAZE

1/2 cup confectioners' sugar

1 tablespoon fresh lime juice

Pineapple and Toasted Coconut Cake

A COUPLE OF RETRO INGREDIENTS—canned pineapple and sweetened flaked coconut—make this a truly enjoyable cake.

MAKE THE CAKE

1. Preheat the oven to 350°F. Grease a 12-cup Bundt pan and dust with flour. Spread the coconut on a baking sheet and toast until just golden, stirring frequently, about 5 minutes. Take care not to burn the coconut. Set aside to cool completely.

2. Combine the eggs, sour cream, and vanilla in a large measuring cup and lightly beat. Combine the flour, baking powder, baking soda, and salt in a medium bowl.

3. Combine the butter and sugar in a large mixing bowl and cream with an electric mixer on medium-high speed until fluffy, about 3 minutes, scraping down the sides of the bowl once or twice as necessary.

4. With the mixer on medium-low speed, pour 1/3 of the egg mixture into the bowl in a slow stream. Add 1/3 of the flour mixture. Add another 1/3 of the egg mixture and another 1/3 of the flour mixture. Add the remaining egg mixture and then the remaining flour mixture. Scrape down the sides of the bowl and beat on medium speed for 1 minute. Stir in the toasted coconut and the pineapple chunks.

5. Scrape the batter into the prepared pan. Bake the cake until a toothpick inserted in the center comes out clean, 1 hour to 1 hour and 10 minutes. Let the cake cool in the pan for 15 minutes, then invert it onto a wire rack to cool completely.

MAKE THE GLAZE

1. Whisk together the confectioners' sugar and lime juice in a medium bowl. Place the cake on a wire rack set over a baking sheet. Drizzle the glaze over the cake, allowing it to run down the sides of the cake. Let the glaze set for 30 minutes before slicing and serving.

2. Store uneaten cake in a cake keeper or wrap in plastic and store at room temperature for up to 3 days.

Whole-Wheat *and* Honey-Nut Bundt Cake

HERE IS A WHOLESOME-TASTING CAKE with good whole-wheat flavor. A honey-buttermilk-caramel glaze gives it country character.

MAKE THE FILLING

1. Combine the flour, butter, and cinnamon in a medium bowl until crumbly. Stir in the nuts and honey. Set aside.

MAKE THE CAKE

1. Preheat the oven to 350°F. Grease a 12-cup Bundt pan and dust with flour. Whisk together the buttermilk, eggs, and vanilla in a large glass measuring cup. Whisk together the white flour, whole-wheat flour, baking powder, baking soda, and salt in a medium bowl.

2. Combine the butter and brown sugar in a large mixing bowl and cream with an electric mixer on medium-high speed until fluffy, about 3 minutes. With the mixer on low speed, add $1/3$ of the flour mixture and beat until incorporated. Add $1/2$ of the buttermilk mixture. Repeat, alternating flour and buttermilk mixtures and ending with the flour mixture, scraping down the sides of the bowl between additions. Beat on high for 1 minute.

3. Scrape half of the batter into the prepared pan. Spoon the filling over the batter. Scrape the remaining batter into the top of the pan and smooth with a spatula. Bake until a toothpick inserted in the center comes out clean, 40 to 45 minutes. Let the cake cool in the pan for 5 minutes, then invert it onto a wire rack to cool completely.

MAKE THE GLAZE

1. Combine the sugar, honey, and buttermilk in a small saucepan and bring to a boil. Turn the heat to medium low and cook, stirring occasionally, until the glaze is caramel colored, 7 to 9 minutes. Remove from the heat, stir in the vanilla, and let cool for 10 minutes. Pour the warm glaze over the cake, letting it drip down the sides. Let stand until the glaze is set, about $1/2$ hour. Slice and serve. Store uneaten cake in a cake keeper or wrap in plastic and store at room temperature for up to 3 days.

Serves 10 to 12

FOR THE FILLING

$1/2$ cup unbleached all-purpose flour

2 tablespoons unsalted butter, softened

1 teaspoon ground cinnamon

$1 1/4$ cups walnuts or pecans, coarsely chopped

$1/2$ cup honey

FOR THE CAKE

1 cup buttermilk

2 large eggs

1 teaspoon pure vanilla extract

$1 1/3$ cups unbleached all-purpose flour

$2/3$ cup whole-wheat flour

1 teaspoon baking powder

1 teaspoon baking soda

$1/2$ teaspoon salt

$1/2$ cup (1 stick) unsalted butter, softened

1 cup packed light brown sugar

FOR THE GLAZE

$1/4$ cup granulated sugar

$1/4$ cup honey

$1/4$ cup buttermilk

$1/2$ teaspoon pure vanilla extract

FOR THE CAKE

1 cup sour cream

3 large eggs

2 teaspoons pure vanilla extract

2 1/4 cups unbleached all-purpose flour

1 teaspoon baking powder

1/2 teaspoon baking soda

1/2 teaspoon salt

1/2 cup (1 stick) unsalted butter, softened

1 cup smooth peanut butter

1 1/2 cups packed light brown sugar

FOR THE GLAZE

8 ounces semisweet or bittersweet chocolate, finely chopped

2 tablespoons unsalted butter

3/4 cup heavy cream

1 Butterfinger bar (60 grams), chopped

Peanut Butter–Sour Cream Bundt Cake with Butterfinger-Ganache Glaze

ACCORDING TO MY FAMILY, this is the best cake in the book with its chocolate glaze and Butterfinger candy bars.

MAKE THE CAKE

1. Preheat the oven to 350°F. Grease a 12-cup Bundt pan and dust with flour. Whisk together the sour cream, eggs, and vanilla in a large glass measuring cup. Whisk together the flour, baking powder, baking soda, and salt in a medium bowl.

2. Combine the butter, peanut butter, and brown sugar in a large mixing bowl and cream with an electric mixer on medium-high speed until fluffy, about 3 minutes, scraping down the sides of the bowl once or twice as necessary.

3. With the mixer on low, add 1/3 of the flour mixture and beat until incorporated. Add 1/2 of the sour cream mixture. Repeat, alternating flour and sour cream mixtures and ending with the flour mixture, scraping down the sides of the bowl between additions. Turn the mixer to medium-high speed and beat for 1 minute.

4. Scrape the batter into the prepared pan. Bake until a toothpick inserted in the center comes out clean, 40 to 45 minutes. Let the cake cool in the pan for 5 minutes, then invert it onto a wire rack to cool completely.

MAKE THE GLAZE

1. Place the chocolate and butter in a heatproof bowl. Heat the cream in a small saucepan over medium-high heat until it comes to a boil. Pour the cream over the chocolate and butter and let stand for 5 minutes. Whisk until smooth.

2. Pour the warm glaze over the cake, letting it drop down the sides. Sprinkle the chopped Butterfinger bar over the glaze. Let stand until the glaze is set, about 1/2 hour. Slice and serve. Store uneaten cake in a cake keeper or wrap in plastic and store at room temperature for up to 3 days.

CHAPTER 5

Crumb Cakes
& Other Cakes Baked in a Springform Pan

Blueberry Buckle— recipe on page 134

Until recently, I only thought about my spring-form pan when I was getting ready to bake a cheesecake, a flourless chocolate cake, or another custard-based cake too delicate and difficult to remove from a conventional cake pan. Then one day last spring, I tried making a rhubarb crumb cake in my plain old round cake pan. I realized what a grave mistake this was when I inverted the cake onto a wire rack, watching in horror as more than half of the crumbs fell off the cake and onto the counter and floor. It would have been a lot smarter to bake a crumb cake in a pan with removable sides, so as to avoid having to turn it upside down.

The recipes in this chapter were inspired by that revelation. Most of them are cakes with crumb or streusel toppings. A couple were conceived with the knowledge that they would be difficult to remove from a regular cake pan because of their delicate crumb (the Coca-Cola® Cake) or pretty topping (the Red Grape Cake) but simple to release from a springform pan.

When I bake a cheesecake, I let it cool completely in the pan, refrigerate it still in the pan, and only release the pan sides when I'm ready to serve it. The pan keeps the cake from drying out as it cools and protects it while it's in the refrigerator. But with the crumb cakes in this chapter, I like to remove the sides of the pan soon after baking and slide the cake from the pan bottom to a wire rack to allow it to cool. This way, steam can escape from the hot cake and won't make the bottom soggy.

FOR THE STREUSEL

1/3 cup unbleached all-purpose flour

1/2 cup packed light brown sugar

1/2 cup granulated sugar

1/4 teaspoon ground cinnamon

1/4 teaspoon salt

4 tablespoons (1/2 stick) unsalted butter, chilled and cut into pieces

FOR THE CAKE

2 cups unbleached all-purpose flour

2 teaspoons baking powder

1/2 teaspoon salt

3 cups blueberries, washed and picked over

4 tablespoons (1/2 stick) unsalted butter, at room temperature

3/4 cup granulated sugar

1 large egg

1 teaspoon pure vanilla extract

1/2 cup milk

Blueberry Buckle

THE BEST THING ABOUT THIS bursting-with-fruit cake is the topping, which gets incredibly crunchy and candy-like during its long stay in a hot oven.

MAKE THE STREUSEL

1. Preheat the oven to 375°F. Grease a 9-inch round springform pan.

2. Combine the flour, brown sugar, granulated sugar, cinnamon, and salt in a large mixing bowl. Add the butter; use an electric mixer to mix, on low, until it resembles coarse meal with some larger crumbs. Transfer to a smaller bowl and refrigerate until ready to use.

MAKE THE CAKE

1. Combine the flour, baking powder, and salt in a medium mixing bowl. Place the berries in a bowl and stir in 1/4 cup of the flour mixture to coat.

2. Combine the butter and granulated sugar in the large mixing bowl and cream with an electric mixer on medium-high speed until fluffy, about 3 minutes, scraping down the sides of the bowl once or twice as necessary. With the mixer on low speed, add the egg and vanilla.

3. With the mixer on low speed, add 1/3 of the flour mixture and then 1/2 of the milk, scraping down the sides of the bowl after each addition. Repeat, alternating flour and milk and ending with flour. Stir in the berry and flour mixture with a large rubber spatula, trying not to mash too many of the berries. The batter will be stiff. Scrape the batter into the prepared pan and smooth into an even layer with a spatula.

4. Squeeze the streusel through your fingers and onto the batter, distributing it evenly over the cake and making some large crumbs. Bake the cake until it is golden and a toothpick inserted in the center comes out clean, 55 to 60 minutes. Let the cake cool in the pan on a wire rack for 10 minutes. Release the sides of the pan and use a large spatula to slide the cake from the pan bottom to a wire rack. Cool completely, cut into wedges, and serve.

5. Store uneaten cake in a cake keeper or wrap in plastic and store at room temperature for up to 2 days.

Cherry-Almond Crumb Cake

ALMOND PASTE GIVES THIS CAKE a tantalizing flavor and extra moisture, so it stays fresh for days. Dried cherries are the perfect fruity match for the almond paste, just as intense but tart rather than sweet.

Serves 8 to 10

FOR THE STREUSEL

1 cup unbleached all-purpose flour

2/3 cup packed light brown sugar

3/4 cup almonds, chopped

1/4 teaspoon salt

6 tablespoons (3/4 stick) unsalted butter, melted

FOR THE CAKE

5 large eggs

1/4 cup milk

2 teaspoons pure vanilla extract

1 1/2 cups unbleached all-purpose flour

1 1/2 teaspoons baking powder

1/4 teaspoon salt

1 cup granulated sugar

1 package (7 ounces) almond paste, cut into small pieces

1 cup (2 sticks) unsalted butter, softened

1 cup dried cherries

MAKE THE STREUSEL

1. Preheat the oven to 300°F. Grease a 10-inch round springform pan.

2. Combine the flour, brown sugar, almonds, salt, and butter in a medium bowl. Work the mixture between your fingers to form large crumbs. Refrigerate until ready to use.

MAKE THE CAKE

1. Combine the eggs, milk, and vanilla in a large glass measuring cup and lightly beat. Combine the flour, baking powder, and salt in a medium mixing bowl.

2. Combine the granulated sugar and almond paste in a large mixing bowl and beat with an electric mixer on medium speed until the almond paste is broken up into sandy pieces. Add the butter and beat on medium-high speed until smooth and fluffy, about 3 minutes, scraping down the sides of the bowl once or twice as necessary.

3. With the mixer on medium-low speed, pour 1/3 of the egg mixture into the bowl in a slow stream. Add 1/3 of the flour mixture. Add another 1/3 of the egg mixture and another 1/3 of the flour mixture. Add the remaining egg mixture and then the remaining flour mixture. Scrape down the sides of the bowl and beat on medium speed for 1 minute. Stir in the cherries.

4. Scrape the batter into the prepared pan, smoothing the top with a spatula. Sprinkle the streusel over the cake and press on it lightly with your fingertips so it adheres to the surface. Bake the cake until it is golden and a toothpick inserted in the center comes out clean, 1 hour to 1 hour and 10 minutes. Let the cake cool in the pan on a wire rack for 10 minutes. Release the sides of the pan and use a large spatula to slide the cake from the pan bottom to a wire rack. Cool completely, cut into wedges, and serve.

5. Store uneaten cake in a cake keeper or wrap in plastic and store at room temperature for up to 5 days.

1/3 cup unbleached
   all-purpose flour

1/2 cup packed light
   brown sugar

1/4 teaspoon salt

4 tablespoons (1/2 stick)
   unsalted butter,
   chilled and cut into
   pieces

1 teaspoon pure vanilla
   extract

FOR THE CAKE

2 cups unbleached
   all-purpose flour

2 teaspoons baking
   powder

1/4 teaspoon baking
   soda

1/2 teaspoon salt

3/4 cup (1 1/2 sticks)
   unsalted butter, at
   room temperature

1 cup granulated sugar

2 large eggs

1 teaspoon grated
   lemon zest

2 teaspoons pure vanilla
   extract

3/4 cup buttermilk

1 3/4 cups mini chocolate
   chips

Chocolate Chip Crumb Cake

A LITTLE BIT OF LEMON ZEST gives this Chocolate Chip Crumb Cake some sparkle and zing. Sprinkle the mini chocolate chips on top of the cake as soon as it comes out of the oven so they melt into the crumbs.

MAKE THE STREUSEL

1. Preheat the oven to 350°F. Grease a 9-inch round springform pan.

2. Combine the flour, brown sugar, and salt in a large mixing bowl. Add the butter and vanilla and work the mixture between your fingers to form large crumbs. Transfer to a smaller bowl and refrigerate until ready to use.

MAKE THE CAKE

1. Combine the flour, baking powder, baking soda, and salt in a medium mixing bowl.

2. Combine the butter and granulated sugar in the large mixing bowl and cream with an electric mixer on medium-high speed until fluffy, scraping down the sides of the bowl as necessary. With the mixer on low, add the eggs, lemon zest, and vanilla.

3. With the mixer on low, add 1/3 of the flour mixture and then 1/2 of the buttermilk, scraping down the sides of the bowl after each addition. Repeat, alternating flour and buttermilk and ending with flour. Stir in 1 cup of the chocolate chips.

4. Scrape the batter into the prepared pan and smooth into an even layer with a spatula.

5. Squeeze the streusel through your fingers and onto the batter, distributing it evenly over the cake and making some large crumbs.

6. Bake the cake until it is golden and a toothpick inserted in the center comes out clean, 55 to 60 minutes. Sprinkle the remaining 3/4 cup chocolate chips over the top of the hot cake. Let the cake cool in the pan on a wire rack for 10 minutes. Release the sides of the pan and use a large spatula to slide the cake from the pan bottom to a wire rack. Cool completely, cut into wedges, and serve.

7. Store uneaten cake in a cake keeper or wrap in plastic and store at room temperature for up to 2 days.

Cranberry Cake

AN ENTIRE BAG OF FRESH cranberries goes into this crumb cake, so I tend to bake it when I have an extra bag in the refrigerator after Thanksgiving. It makes a satisfying snack or brunch cake when the apple and pumpkin pies are gone.

MAKE THE STREUSEL

1. Preheat the oven to 300°F. Grease a 10-inch round springform pan.

2. Combine the almonds, butter, and brown sugar in a medium bowl. Work the mixture between your fingers to form large crumbs. Refrigerate until ready to use.

MAKE THE CAKE

1. Whisk together the flour, baking powder, and salt in a medium bowl. Combine the eggs and granulated sugar in a large mixing bowl and beat with an electric mixer on medium-high speed until the mixture is lightened and increased in volume, about 5 minutes. With the mixer on low, add the butter in a slow stream. Turn the mixer to medium speed and beat for another 2 minutes. Stir in the vanilla.

2. Gently but thoroughly fold in the flour mixture, 1/2 cup at a time. Stir in the cranberries.

3. Scrape the batter into the prepared pan, smoothing the top with a spatula. Sprinkle the streusel over the batter. Bake the cake until it is golden and a toothpick inserted in the center comes out clean, 1 hour to 1 hour and 10 minutes. Let the cake cool in the pan on a wire rack for 10 minutes. Release the sides of the pan and use a large spatula to slide the cake from the pan bottom to a wire rack. Cool completely, cut into wedges, and serve.

4. Store uneaten cake in a cake keeper or wrap in plastic and store at room temperature for up to 5 days.

Serves 8 to 10

FOR THE STREUSEL

1 cup sliced almonds

2 tablespoons unsalted butter, melted

2 tablespoons packed light brown sugar

FOR THE CAKE

2 cups unbleached all-purpose flour

1 teaspoon baking powder

1/4 teaspoon salt

3 large eggs

2 cups granulated sugar

3/4 cup (1 1/2 sticks) butter, melted and cooled

1 teaspoon pure vanilla extract

1 bag (12 ounces) fresh cranberries

FOR THE TOPPING

1 cup plus 1 tablespoon sugar

½ teaspoon ground cinnamon

⅓ cup walnuts or pecans, finely chopped

FOR THE CAKE

1 cup unbleached all-purpose flour

1 teaspoon baking powder

¼ teaspoon salt

1 cup sugar

½ cup (1 stick) unsalted butter, softened

2 large eggs

½ teaspoon pure vanilla extract

5 medium ripe nectarines, halved, pitted, and peeled

Nectarine Cake
with Cinnamon-Nut Topping

A THIN LAYER OF RICH CAKE absorbs the juices from ripe nectarine halves. To provide a little crunch, there's a layer of chopped nuts and cinnamon sugar sprinkled on top. You can use any stone fruit in this recipe—plums, apricots, peaches. And for a more rustic (and even quicker) version, skip peeling the fruit.

MAKE THE TOPPING

1. Preheat the oven to 375°F. Grease the inside of a 10-inch round springform pan.

2. Combine 1 tablespoon sugar, the cinnamon, and the nuts in a small bowl. Set aside.

MAKE THE CAKE

1. Combine the flour, baking powder, and salt in a medium mixing bowl.

2. Combine the sugar and butter in a large mixing bowl and cream with an electric mixer on medium-high speed until fluffy, about 3 minutes, scraping down the sides of the bowl once or twice as necessary. With the mixer on low, add the eggs one at a time, scraping down the sides of the bowl after each addition. Stir in the vanilla. Add the flour mixture, ½ cup at a time, scraping down the sides of the bowl after each addition.

3. Scrape the batter into the prepared pan and smooth the top with a rubber spatula. Arrange the nectarines, cut side down, on top of the batter. Sprinkle with the topping. Bake the cake until it is golden and a toothpick inserted in the center comes out clean, 50 to 55 minutes. Let the cake cool in the pan on a wire rack for 10 minutes. Release the sides of the pan and use a large spatula to slide the cake from the pan bottom to a wire rack. Cool completely, cut into wedges, and serve.

4. Store uneaten cake in a cake keeper or wrap in plastic and store at room temperature for up to 2 days.

1¾ cups unbleached all-purpose flour

1 cup granulated sugar

1 cup packed light brown sugar

¾ cup unsweetened Dutch process cocoa powder

2 teaspoons baking powder

¼ teaspoon baking soda

¼ teaspoon salt

2 large eggs

1 cup sour cream

½ cup vegetable oil

1 cup Coca-Cola

1 teaspoon pure vanilla extract

Confectioners' sugar for dusting

Coca-Cola Chocolate Cake

HOW COULD I NOT INCLUDE a version of this southern specialty in a book on simple cakes? The first time I made it, I underbaked it, so that some gooey, warm batter spilled out of the center of every slice. My children loved it! If you want to serve it this way, bake the cake for only 45 minutes and let it stand in the pan for 10 minutes before serving. But if you want it to firm up all the way through, let it go for the recommended baking time.

1. Preheat the oven to 350°F. Grease the inside of a 9-inch round springform pan.

2. Whisk together the flour, granulated sugar, light brown sugar, cocoa powder, baking powder, baking soda, and salt in a large mixing bowl. Whisk together the eggs, sour cream, oil, Coca-Cola, and vanilla in a medium mixing bowl.

3. With a wooden spoon, stir the Coca-Cola mixture into the flour mixture until just combined. Do not overmix.

4. Pour the batter into the prepared pan. Bake until a toothpick inserted in the center of the cake comes out clean, 55 minutes to 1 hour.

5. Set the pan on a wire rack and let cool for 5 minutes. Run a paring knife around the perimeter of the pan to loosen the cake from the pan sides, and release the sides. Use a large spatula to slide the cake from the pan bottom to a wire rack. Let cool completely. Dust heavily with confectioners' sugar, cut into wedges, and serve.

6. Store uneaten cake in a cake keeper or wrap in plastic and store at room temperature for up to 3 days.

Coffee—Heath Bar Crunch Cake

HERE'S A CAKE INSPIRED by a favorite ice cream flavor. The cake is flavored with espresso powder, and the crumbs are made with chopped toffee candy bars. Prechopped toffee bits are sometimes available in the baking aisle of the supermarket. Use 1 cup in place of the candy bars if you'd like.

MAKE THE STREUSEL

1. Preheat the oven to 350°F. Grease a 9-inch round springform pan.

2. Combine the Heath bars, brown sugar, flour, and butter in a medium mixing bowl. Work the mixture with your fingers until it resembles large crumbs. Refrigerate until ready to use.

MAKE THE CAKE

1. Combine the flour, espresso powder, baking powder, and salt in a medium mixing bowl.

2. Combine the butter and brown sugar in a large mixing bowl and cream with an electric mixer on medium-high speed until fluffy, about 3 minutes, scraping down the sides of the bowl once or twice as necessary. With the mixer on low speed, add the egg, egg yolk, and vanilla.

3. With the mixer on low speed, add $1/3$ of the flour mixture and then $1/2$ of the milk, scraping down the sides of the bowl after each addition. Repeat, alternating flour and milk and ending with flour.

4. Scrape the batter into the prepared pan and smooth into an even layer with a spatula. Scatter the streusel onto the batter, distributing it evenly over the cake.

5. Bake the cake until it is golden and a toothpick inserted in the center comes out clean, 55 to 60 minutes. Let the cake cool in the pan on a wire rack for 5 minutes. Release the sides of the pan and use a large spatula to slide the cake from the pan bottom to a wire rack. Cool completely, cut into wedges, and serve.

6. Store uneaten cake in a cake keeper or wrap in plastic and store at room temperature for up to 3 days.

Serves 8 to 10

FOR THE STREUSEL

4 Heath® bars (1.4 ounces each), chopped

2 tablespoons packed light brown sugar

2 tablespoons unbleached all-purpose flour

1 tablespoon butter, softened

FOR THE CAKE

$1^1/2$ cups unbleached all-purpose flour

1 tablespoon instant espresso powder

$1^1/2$ teaspoons baking powder

$1/2$ teaspoon salt

$1/2$ cup (1 stick) unsalted butter, softened

1 cup packed light brown sugar

1 large egg

1 large egg yolk

$1^1/2$ teaspoons pure vanilla extract

1 cup milk

FOR THE CRUMBS

1/2 cup smooth peanut butter

1/4 cup unbleached all-purpose flour

1/4 cup light brown sugar

1/4 cup dry-roasted salted peanuts, chopped

FOR THE CAKE

2 large eggs

1/2 cup whole milk

1 teaspoon pure vanilla extract

1 1/3 cups unbleached all-purpose flour

1 teaspoon baking powder

1/2 teaspoon salt

1/2 cup (1 stick) unsalted butter, softened

3/4 cup granulated sugar

3/4 cup jam

Peanut Butter and Jelly Crumb Cake

THERE'S NO BETTER after-school snack than this kid-friendly crumb cake, handy when your audience might be skeptical about rhubarb or cranberries. Apricot jelly is my personal favorite, but grape jelly gives the cake a classic, nostalgic flavor.

MAKE THE CRUMBS

1. Preheat the oven to 375°F. Grease the inside of a 10-inch round springform pan.

2. Combine the peanut butter, flour, brown sugar, and peanuts in a mixing bowl. Work the mixture between your fingers to form large crumbs. Refrigerate until ready to use.

MAKE THE CAKE

1. Whisk together the eggs, milk, and vanilla in a large measuring cup.

2. Combine the flour, baking powder, and salt in a medium mixing bowl.

3. Combine the butter and sugar in a large mixing bowl and cream with an electric mixer on medium-high until fluffy, scraping down the sides of the bowl as necessary. With the mixer on low speed, slowly add the egg mixture and mix until well combined. Add the flour mixture, 1/2 cup at a time, scraping down the sides of the bowl after each addition.

4. Scrape the batter into the prepared pan and smooth the top with a rubber spatula. Place the jam in a small bowl and whisk until loosened and spreadable. Use a small offset spatula to spread the jam over the batter. Break the peanut butter mixture up into large crumbs with your fingers and drop them over the jam. Bake the cake until it is golden and a toothpick inserted in the center comes out clean, 40 to 45 minutes. Let the cake cool in the pan for about 10 minutes. Release the sides of the pan and use a large spatula to slide the cake from the pan bottom to a wire rack. Cool completely, cut into wedges, and serve.

5. Store uneaten cake in a cake keeper or wrap in plastic and store at room temperature for up to 2 days.

FOR THE STREUSEL

¾ cup unbleached all-purpose flour

⅔ cup packed light brown sugar

½ teaspoon ground cinnamon

¼ teaspoon salt

5 tablespoons unsalted butter, cut into bits, chilled

FOR THE CAKE

½ pound fresh rhubarb stalks, tough strings removed, cut into ¼-inch dice

3 tablespoons confectioners' sugar

2 large eggs

½ cup whole milk

1 teaspoon pure vanilla extract

1⅓ cups unbleached all-purpose flour

1 teaspoon baking powder

½ teaspoon salt

½ cup (1 stick) unsalted butter, softened

¾ cup granulated sugar

Rhubarb Streusel Snacking Cake

MY FAMILY BELONGS to a local community farm where we harvest our own vegetables beginning in June. The first week or two I can always count on bright red and pale green rhubarb. I try to pick slender stalks with no strings, but if yours are thicker and a bit older, be sure to peel away the outer layer of strings before chopping the rhubarb.

MAKE THE STREUSEL

1. Preheat the oven to 375°F. Grease the inside of a 10-inch round springform pan.

2. Combine the flour, brown sugar, cinnamon, and salt in a mixing bowl. Add the butter. Work the mixture between your fingers to form large crumbs. Refrigerate until ready to use.

MAKE THE CAKE

1. Toss the rhubarb with the confectioners' sugar and set aside. Whisk together the eggs, milk, and vanilla in a large measuring cup. Combine the flour, baking powder, and salt in a medium mixing bowl.

2. Combine the butter and granulated sugar in a large mixing bowl and cream with an electric mixer on medium-high speed until fluffy, about 3 minutes, scraping down the sides of the bowl once or twice as necessary. With the mixer on low speed, slowly add the egg mixture and mix until well combined, scraping down the sides of the bowl once or twice as necessary. Add the flour mixture, ½ cup at a time, scraping down the sides of the bowl after each addition.

3. Scrape the batter into the prepared pan and smooth the top with a rubber spatula. Scatter the rhubarb over the batter. Scatter the streusel over the rhubarb. Bake the cake until it is golden and a toothpick inserted in the center comes out clean, 45 to 50 minutes. Let the cake cool in the pan for about 10 minutes. Release the sides of the pan and use a large spatula to slide the cake from the pan bottom to a wire rack. Cool completely, cut into wedges, and serve. Store uneaten cake in a cake keeper or wrap in plastic and store at room temperature for up to 2 days.

1 cup unbleached
all-purpose flour

1/2 cup yellow cornmeal

1 1/2 teaspoons baking
powder

1/4 teaspoon salt

2 large eggs

2/3 cup sugar

1/2 cup extra-virgin
olive oil

1/3 cup milk

1 teaspoon pure vanilla
extract

1 teaspoon grated
lemon zest

1 3/4 cups (about
10 ounces) red
seedless grapes,
washed and dried

Confectioners' sugar
for dusting

Red Grape, Polenta, and Olive Oil Cake

HERE IS A RUSTIC Italian-style cake, fragrant from olive oil and juicy with roasted grapes. If you add all the grapes at once, they'll sink to the bottom, so reserve half and scatter them on top of the cake after it's been in the oven for 10 minutes. They'll sink slightly but still be visible. Dust the cake with confectioners' sugar before serving for a pretty presentation. If it is a dinner party dessert, serve it with an Italian sweet wine like Vin Santo or with small glasses of grappa.

1. Preheat the oven to 350°F. Grease a 9-inch round springform pan. Whisk together the flour, cornmeal, baking powder, and salt in a medium bowl.

2. Combine the eggs and sugar in a large mixing bowl. Beat on medium-high speed until light in color and increased in volume, about 5 minutes. With the mixer on low speed, add the oil in a slow, steady stream. Turn the mixer to medium speed and beat for 1 minute. Stir in the milk, vanilla, and lemon zest on low speed.

3. With the mixer on low speed, add the flour mixture, 1/2 cup at a time, until just incorporated. Stir in 1/2 of the grapes. Scrape the batter into the prepared pan and bake for 10 minutes.

4. Scatter the remaining grapes over the top of the partially baked cake and continue to bake until the cake is golden and a toothpick inserted in the center of the cake comes out clean, about 40 minutes longer.

5. Transfer the pan to a wire rack and let cool for 5 minutes. Release the sides from the pan and let the cake cool completely before dusting with confectioners' sugar, cutting into wedges, and serving.

6. Store uneaten cake in a cake keeper or wrap in plastic and store at room temperature for up to 3 days.

CHAPTER 6

Angel Food
& Chiffon Cakes

Lime Chiffon Cake—recipe on page 162

Compared to the "shortened" cakes of the previous chapter, which are buttery and satisfyingly filling, angel food and chiffon cakes, or "foam cakes," are sweet and ethereal. Angel food cake is the leanest and lightest of all cakes. It has no oil, no egg yolks, and no chemical leaveners. Egg whites and sugar are beaten together to form a meringue, into which some flour is folded. Chiffon cakes do contain whole eggs, some oil, and a little baking powder, but they also rely primarily on a meringue folded into the batter for their lofty height.

When making a foam cake, you must whip your egg whites with care. Use chilled egg whites, which will whip up higher than room-temperature whites. For angel food cake, beat the whites on low speed to break them up. Add some cream of tartar, which will help the whites keep their shape, and whip until the egg whites are cloudlike and soft. With the mixer still on, add the sugar in a very slow stream until the whites are shiny and hold soft peaks. Don't overwhip your whites when making angel food cake, or you will have difficulty folding in the dry ingredients without deflating them.

For chiffon cakes, beat the whites until they hold very stiff peaks. If the whites aren't whipped sufficiently, the cake will be damp on the bottom and flat.

For the most tender angel food and chiffon cakes, use low-protein cake flour instead of all-purpose flour.

These cakes must be baked in a tube pan with tall sides and metal "feet" that extend from the top edge of the pan. These features let the cake reach and maintain its full volume. The tube shape conducts heat to the batter efficiently, allowing the cake to rise quickly before the air bubbles beaten into the batter can deflate. When you remove the cake from the oven, turn the pan upside down and set it on its feet. Air will be able to circulate underneath the cake so it won't become soggy, and gravity will prevent it from shrinking as it cools.

FOR THE CAKE

1 cup cake flour

1½ cups sugar

¼ teaspoon salt

1 tablespoon plus
   1 teaspoon instant
   espresso powder

12 large egg whites

1 teaspoon cream of
   tartar

2 teaspoons pure vanilla
   extract

FOR THE GLAZE

6 tablespoons (¾ stick)
   unsalted butter, cut
   into 6 pieces

6 tablespoons firmly
   packed light brown
   sugar

2 teaspoons instant
   espresso powder

6 tablespoons heavy
   cream

1½ cups confectioners'
   sugar

2 tablespoons hazelnut
   liqueur, such as
   Frangelico®

Coffee Angel Food Cake
with Hazelnut-Coffee Glaze

I LOVE THE WAY a little instant espresso powder gives a bitter edge to angel food cake. Other liqueurs (Grand Marnier is good) or liquors (bourbon or dark rum) could replace the Frangelico in the glaze, or you could leave it out altogether if you prefer.

MAKE THE CAKE

1. Preheat the oven to 325°F. Have ready a 9-inch ungreased angel food tube pan with a removable bottom.

2. Combine the flour, ¾ cup sugar, salt, and instant espresso powder in a medium mixing bowl and whisk thoroughly to break up any lumps. Set aside.

3. Place the egg whites in a large mixing bowl and whip them with an electric mixer fitted with a whisk attachment on medium speed until frothy. Add the cream of tartar and continue to beat on medium speed until the egg whites begin to turn white. With the mixer still on medium speed, pour in the remaining ¾ cup sugar in a slow, steady stream and whip until the whites are shiny white and just hold soft, floppy peaks when the whisk is lifted from the mixture. Stir in the vanilla until just mixed in.

4. Place a small fine-mesh strainer over the bowl of egg whites and strain about ¼ cup of the flour mixture into the egg white mixture. Gently fold in the flour mixture with a rubber spatula. Repeat with the remaining flour mixture in ¼-cup increments until all of it has been folded in. Pour the batter into the tube pan and smooth the top with a rubber spatula. Bake the cake until it is golden brown and the top springs back when you touch it, about 50 minutes.

5. Remove the pan from the oven. If your pan has feet, invert the pan onto a heatproof surface and allow it to cool. If your pan doesn't have feet, invert 4 heatproof drinking glasses on the counter and rest the inverted pan on top of the glasses to allow air to circulate around the cake while it cools. Let the cake cool in the pan for at least 1 hour or for up to 6 hours.

MAKE THE GLAZE

1. Stir the butter, brown sugar, and espresso powder together in a small saucepan over medium heat until the butter melts. Stir in the heavy cream. Simmer for 1 minute. Remove from the heat. Gradually add the confectioners' sugar, whisking until smooth. Whisk in the liqueur. Let cool to warm room temperature.

2. To remove the cake from the pan, run a sharp paring knife around the edges, being careful to leave the golden crust intact. Remove the sides of the pan. Invert the cake onto a serving platter. Run the paring knife under the removable bottom of the pan and lift it off the cake. Drizzle the glaze over the cake and let stand for 30 minutes to set before serving.

3. Store uneaten cake in a cake keeper or wrap in plastic and store at room temperature for up to 3 days.

FOR THE CAKE

1¼ cups cake flour

1½ cups packed light brown sugar

¼ teaspoon salt

14 large egg whites

1 teaspoon cream of tartar

2 teaspoons pure vanilla extract

FOR THE GLAZE

1 cup confectioners' sugar

1 teaspoon ground cinnamon

2 tablespoons milk

Brown Sugar Angel Food Cake

ANGEL FOOD CAKE MADE with brown sugar has a little more character than the pure white variety. It makes a beautiful base for ice cream and fresh fruit—coffee ice cream and fresh figs is my favorite combination.

MAKE THE CAKE

1. Preheat the oven to 350°F. Have ready a 9-inch ungreased angel food tube pan with a removable bottom.

2. Combine the flour, ¾ cup brown sugar, and salt in a medium mixing bowl and whisk thoroughly to break up any lumps. Set aside.

3. Place the egg whites in a large mixing bowl and whip them with an electric mixer fitted with a whisk attachment on medium speed until frothy. Add the cream of tartar and continue to beat on medium speed until the egg whites begin to turn white. With the mixer still on medium speed, pour in the remaining ¾ cup brown sugar in a slow, steady stream and whip until the egg whites just hold soft, floppy peaks when the whisk is lifted from the mixture. Stir in the vanilla until just mixed in.

4. Place a small fine-mesh strainer over the bowl of egg whites and strain about ¼ cup of the flour mixture into the egg white mixture. Gently fold in the flour mixture with a rubber spatula. Repeat with the remaining flour mixture in ¼-cup increments until all of it has been folded in. Pour the batter into the tube pan and smooth the top with a rubber spatula. Bake the cake until it is golden brown and the top springs back when you touch it, about 45 minutes.

5. Remove the pan from the oven. If your pan has feet, invert the pan onto a heatproof surface and allow it to cool. If your pan doesn't have feet, invert 4 heatproof drinking glasses on the counter and rest the inverted pan on top of the glasses to allow air to circulate around the cake while it cools. Let the cake cool in the pan for at least 1 hour or for up to 6 hours.

MAKE THE GLAZE

1. In a medium bowl, whisk together the confectioners' sugar, cinnamon, and milk until smooth.

2. To remove the cake from the pan, run a sharp paring knife around the edges, being careful to leave the golden crust intact. Remove the sides of the pan. Invert the cake onto a serving platter. Run the paring knife under the removable bottom of the pan and lift it off the cake. Drizzle the glaze over the cake and let stand for 30 minutes to set before serving.

3. Store uneaten cake in a cake keeper or wrap in plastic and store at room temperature for up to 3 days.

9 tablespoons cake flour

3 tablespoons unsweetened Dutch process cocoa powder

1 1/2 cups sugar

1/4 teaspoon salt

12 large egg whites

1 teaspoon cream of tartar

2 teaspoons pure vanilla extract

1/2 cup mini chocolate chips

Cocoa-Chip Angel Food Cake

TOO OFTEN, RECIPES FOR CHOCOLATE angel food cake have an anemic chocolate flavor. To boost the chocolate quotient, fold a half cup of mini chocolate chips into the cocoa batter. For a light accompaniment, serve with sweetened raspberries.

1. Preheat the oven to 325°F. Have ready a 9-inch ungreased angel food tube pan with a removable bottom. Combine the flour, cocoa powder, 3/4 cup sugar, and salt in a medium mixing bowl and whisk thoroughly to break up any lumps. Set aside.

2. Place the egg whites in a large mixing bowl and whip them with an electric mixer fitted with a whisk attachment on medium speed until frothy. Add the cream of tartar and continue to beat on medium speed until the egg whites begin to turn white. With the mixer still on medium speed, pour in the remaining 3/4 cup sugar in a slow, steady stream and whip until the whites are shiny white and just hold soft, floppy peaks when the whisk is lifted from the mixture. Stir in the vanilla.

3. Place a small fine-mesh strainer over the bowl of egg whites and strain about 1/4 cup of the flour mixture into the egg white mixture. Gently fold in the flour mixture with a rubber spatula. Repeat with the remaining flour mixture in 1/4-cup increments until all of it has been folded in. Fold in the chocolate chips. Pour the batter into the tube pan and smooth the top with a rubber spatula. Bake the cake until the top springs back when you touch it, about 50 minutes.

4. Remove the pan from the oven. If your pan has feet, invert the pan onto a heatproof surface and allow it to cool. If your pan doesn't have feet, invert 4 heatproof drinking glasses on the counter and rest the inverted pan on top of the glasses to allow air to circulate around the cake while it cools. Let the cake cool in the pan for at least 1 hour or for up to 6 hours.

5. To remove the cake from the pan, run a sharp paring knife around the edges, being careful to leave the golden crust intact. Remove the sides of the pan. Invert the cake onto a serving platter. Run the paring knife under the removable bottom of the pan and lift it off the cake.

6. Store uneaten cake in a cake keeper or wrap in plastic and store at room temperature for up to 3 days.

½ cup sweetened flaked coconut

1 cup cake flour

1½ cups sugar

¼ teaspoon salt

12 large egg whites

1 teaspoon cream of tartar

2 teaspoons pure vanilla extract

1 teaspoon coconut extract

Coconut Angel Food Cake

SERVE SLICES OF THIS CAKE with fruit sorbet or with some diced mango and pineapple sprinkled with rum and sugar.

1. Preheat the oven to 325°F. Have ready a 9-inch ungreased angel food tube pan with a removable bottom. Place the coconut in the bowl of a food processor and process until finely ground. Set aside. Combine the flour, ¾ cup sugar, and salt in a medium mixing bowl and whisk thoroughly to break up any lumps. Set aside.

2. Place the egg whites in a large mixing bowl and whip them with an electric mixer fitted with a whisk attachment on medium speed until frothy. Add the cream of tartar and continue to beat on medium speed until the egg whites begin to turn white. With the mixer still on medium speed, pour in the remaining ¾ cup sugar in a slow, steady stream and whip until the whites are shiny white and just hold soft, floppy peaks when the whisk is lifted from the mixture. Stir in the vanilla and coconut extracts until just mixed in.

3. Place a small fine-mesh strainer over the bowl of egg whites and strain about ¼ cup of the flour mixture into the egg white mixture. Gently fold in the flour mixture with a rubber spatula. Repeat with the remaining flour mixture in ¼-cup increments until all of it has been folded in. Gently fold in the coconut. Pour the batter into the tube pan and smooth the top with a rubber spatula. Bake the cake until it is golden brown, about 50 minutes.

4. Remove the pan from the oven. If your pan has feet, invert the pan onto a heatproof surface and allow it to cool. If your pan doesn't have feet, invert 4 heatproof drinking glasses on the counter and rest the inverted pan on top of the glasses to allow air to circulate around the cake while it cools. Let the cake cool in the pan for at least 1 hour or for up to 6 hours.

5. To remove the cake from the pan, run a sharp paring knife around the edges, being careful to leave the golden crust intact. Remove the sides of the pan. Invert the cake onto a serving platter. Run the paring knife under the removable bottom of the pan and lift it off the cake. Slice and serve. Store uneaten cake in a cake keeper or wrap in plastic and store at room temperature for up to 3 days.

Lemon Poppy Seed Angel Food Cake *with Lemon–Cream Cheese Glaze*

JUST A TABLESPOON OF POPPY SEEDS is enough to speckle the cake without weighing it down. The glaze is optional, but it adds wonderful richness to the lighter-than-air cake.

MAKE THE CAKE

1. Preheat the oven to 325°F. Have ready a 9-inch ungreased angel food tube pan with a removable bottom.

2. Combine the flour, 3/4 cup sugar, and salt in a medium mixing bowl and whisk thoroughly to break up any lumps. Set aside.

3. Place the egg whites in a large mixing bowl and whip them with an electric mixer fitted with a whisk attachment on medium speed until frothy. Add the cream of tartar and continue to beat on medium speed until the egg whites begin to turn white. With the mixer still on medium speed, pour in the remaining 3/4 cup sugar in a slow, steady stream and whip until the whites are shiny white and just hold soft, floppy peaks when the whisk is lifted from the mixture. Stir in the zest, poppy seeds, and lemon and vanilla extracts until just mixed in.

4. Place a small fine-mesh strainer over the bowl of egg whites and strain about 1/4 cup of the flour mixture into the egg white mixture. Gently fold in the flour mixture with a rubber spatula. Repeat with the remaining flour mixture in 1/4-cup increments until all of it has been folded in. Pour the batter into the tube pan and smooth the top with a rubber spatula. Bake the cake until it is golden brown and the top springs back when you touch it, about 50 minutes.

5. Remove the pan from the oven. If your pan has feet, invert the pan onto a heatproof surface and allow it to cool. If your pan doesn't have feet, invert 4 heatproof drinking glasses on the counter and rest the inverted pan on top of

continued on page 159

FOR THE CAKE

1 cup cake flour

1 1/2 cups sugar

1/4 teaspoon salt

12 large egg whites

1 teaspoon cream of tartar

1 1/2 teaspoons grated lemon zest

1 tablespoon poppy seeds

1/2 teaspoon pure lemon extract

1/2 teaspoon pure vanilla extract

FOR THE GLAZE

6 ounces cream cheese, softened

2 tablespoons fresh lemon juice

2 teaspoons grated lemon zest

1/2 teaspoon pure vanilla extract

1/2 cup heavy cream

1 1/4 cups confectioners' sugar

continued from page 157

the glasses to allow air to circulate around the cake while it cools. Let the cake cool in the pan for at least 1 hour or for up to 6 hours.

MAKE THE GLAZE

1. Combine the cream cheese, lemon juice, lemon zest, vanilla, heavy cream, and confectioners' sugar in the bowl of a food processor and blend until smooth, scraping down the sides of the bowl once or twice as necessary.

2. To remove the cake from the pan, run a sharp paring knife around the edges, being careful to leave the golden crust intact. Remove the sides of the pan. Invert the cake onto a serving platter. Run the paring knife under the removable bottom of the pan and lift it off the cake. Drizzle the glaze over the cake and let stand for 30 minutes to set before slicing and serving.

3. Store uneaten cake in a cake keeper or wrap in plastic and store at room temperature for up to 3 days.

1 1/3 cups cake flour

2 teaspoons baking
    powder

1 1/2 teaspoons ground
    cinnamon

1/4 teaspoon ground
    cloves

1/2 teaspoon salt

7 large eggs,
    5 separated, 2 left
    whole

1 1/2 cups sugar

1/2 cup vegetable oil

1 teaspoon pure vanilla
    extract

2/3 cup water

1/2 cup finely chopped
    walnuts or pecans

1/4 teaspoon
    cream of tartar

Cinnamon-Nut Chiffon Cake

THIS IS A SIMPLE WAY to add satisfying flavor to a plain chiffon cake. Chop the nuts finely so they won't weigh down your batter. But take care, if you are chopping the nuts in a food processor, that they don't become oily, which will compromise the meringue and prevent your cake from rising fully.

1. Preheat the oven to 325°F. Have ready a 9-inch ungreased angel food tube pan with a removable bottom.

2. Combine the flour, baking powder, cinnamon, cloves, and salt in a medium bowl and whisk thoroughly to break up any lumps. Set aside.

3. Place the egg yolks and whole eggs in a large mixing bowl and beat on medium-high speed until lightened in color, about 3 minutes. With the mixer running, add 1 cup sugar in a slow, steady stream and continue to beat until the mixture is light and increased in volume, about 5 minutes longer. With the mixer still running, slowly pour in the oil and continue to beat for 1 minute longer. Stir in the vanilla.

4. With the mixer on low speed, add 1/3 of the flour mixture, then 1/2 of the water, then the remaining flour mixture, scraping down the bowl once or twice as necessary. Stir in the nuts.

5. With clean beaters and using a clean mixing bowl, whip the egg whites on medium speed until frothy. Add the cream of tartar and continue to beat on medium speed until the egg whites begin to turn white. With the mixer still on medium speed, pour in the remaining 1/2 cup sugar in a slow, steady stream and whip until the whites hold stiff peaks.

6. Fold 1/4 of the yolk mixture into the whites to lighten. Then fold the whites into the yolk mixture, gently but thoroughly. Pour the batter into the tube pan and smooth the top with a rubber spatula. Bake the cake until it is golden brown and the top springs back when you touch it, 55 minutes to 1 hour.

7. Remove the pan from the oven. If your pan has feet, invert the pan onto a heatproof surface and allow it to cool. If your pan doesn't have feet, invert 4 heatproof drinking glasses on the counter and rest the inverted pan on top of

the glasses to allow air to circulate around the cake while it cools. Let the cake cool in the pan completely, about 2 hours.

8. To remove the cake from the pan, run a sharp paring knife around the edges, being careful to leave the golden crust intact. Remove the sides of the pan. Invert the cake onto a serving platter. Run the paring knife under the removable bottom of the pan and lift it off the cake. Slice and serve.

9. Store uneaten cake in a cake keeper or wrap in plastic and store at room temperature for up to 3 days.

Using Leftover Egg Yolks

AFTER BAKING QUITE A FEW angel food cakes while working on this book, I came up with a good list of recipes to help use up my extra egg yolks. In addition to baking a Rich Yellow Loaf Cake (page 94), you could make any of the following:

CRÈME ANGLAISE A custard sauce that's delicious served alongside cake. Be very efficient and serve it with your angel food cake.

CRÈME BRÛLÉE A typical recipe calls for 1 egg yolk per serving.

EGGNOG 12 egg yolks and 2 quarts of half-and-half will get you 8 servings of Christmas cheer. For optimum enjoyment, don't think about cholesterol.

MAYONNAISE Homemade mayonnaise can be flavored with garlic, spices, or herbs and has a million different uses.

1⅓ cups cake flour

½ teaspoon baking soda

½ teaspoon salt

7 large eggs, 5 separated, 2 left whole

1½ cups sugar

½ cup vegetable oil

⅓ cup fresh lime juice

⅓ cup water

2 teaspoons grated lime zest

1 teaspoon pure vanilla extract

⅓ teaspoon cream of tartar

Lime Chiffon Cake

THIS BRIGHT-TASTING CHIFFON cake is a great foil for fresh tropical fruit. Try it alongside pineapple chunks tossed with a little sugar and grated fresh ginger.

1. Preheat the oven to 325°F. Have ready a 9-inch ungreased angel food tube pan with a removable bottom.

2. Combine the flour, baking soda, and salt in a medium bowl and whisk thoroughly to break up any lumps. Set aside.

3. Place the egg yolks and whole eggs in a large mixing bowl and beat on medium-high speed until lightened in color, about 3 minutes. With the mixer running, add 1 cup sugar in a slow, steady stream and continue to beat until the mixture is light and increased in volume, about 5 minutes longer. With the mixer still running, slowly pour in the oil and continue to beat for 1 minute longer.

4. Combine the lime juice and water in a measuring cup. With the mixer on low speed, add ⅓ of the flour mixture, then ½ the lime juice and water mixture, then another ⅓ of the flour mixture, the remaining lime juice and water mixture, and the remaining flour mixture, scraping down the bowl once or twice as necessary. Stir in the lime zest and vanilla.

5. With clean beaters and using a clean mixing bowl, whip the egg whites on medium speed until frothy. Add the cream of tartar and continue to beat on medium speed until the egg whites begin to turn white. With the mixer still on medium speed, pour in the remaining ½ cup sugar in a slow, steady stream and whip until the whites hold stiff peaks.

6. Fold ¼ of the yolk mixture into the whites to lighten. Then fold the remaining whites into the yolk mixture, gently but thoroughly. Pour the batter into the tube pan and smooth the top with a rubber spatula. Bake the cake until it is golden brown and the top springs back when you touch it, 55 minutes to 1 hour.

7. Remove the pan from the oven. If your pan has feet, invert the pan onto a heatproof surface and allow it to cool. If your pan doesn't have feet, invert 4 heatproof drinking glasses on the counter and rest the inverted pan on top of

the glasses to allow air to circulate around the cake while it cools. Let the cake cool in the pan completely, about 2 hours.

8. To remove the cake from the pan, run a sharp paring knife around the edges, being careful to leave the golden crust intact. Remove the sides of the pan. Invert the cake onto a serving platter. Run the paring knife under the removable bottom of the pan and lift it off the cake. Slice and serve.

9. Store uneaten cake in a cake keeper or wrap in plastic and store at room temperature for up to 3 days.

1⅓ cups cake flour

2 teaspoons baking
   powder

½ teaspoon salt

7 large eggs,
   5 separated, 2 left
   whole

1½ cups sugar

½ cup vegetable oil

1 whole vanilla bean

⅔ cup water

¼ teaspoon
   cream of tartar

Vanilla Bean Chiffon Cake

THIS IS A RECIPE FOR THE SIMPLEST OF LUXURIES, a chiffon cake flavored with the seeds from a whole vanilla bean. If you've never tried this, you will be amazed at the intensity of flavor you get. Buy only plump, moist beans from specialty foods stores where there is a high turnover, or order them online from www.kingarthurflour.com. Store them in an airtight container or zipper-top bag at room temperature (refrigeration will cause them to grow moldy) for up to 2 years.

1. Preheat the oven to 325°F. Have ready a 9-inch ungreased angel food tube pan with a removable bottom.

2. Combine the flour, baking powder, and salt in a medium bowl and whisk thoroughly to break up any lumps. Set aside.

3. Place the egg yolks and whole eggs in a large mixing bowl and beat on medium-high speed until lightened in color, about 3 minutes. With the mixer running, add 1 cup sugar in a slow, steady stream and continue to beat until the mixture is light and increased in volume, about 5 minutes longer. With the mixer still running, slowly pour in the oil and continue to beat for 1 minute longer. Use a sharp paring knife to split the vanilla bean lengthwise. Use the edge of the knife to scrape the seeds from the bean and into the bowl. Stir to distribute.

4. With the mixer on low speed, add ⅓ of the flour mixture, then ½ the water. Repeat, ending with the flour mixture, scraping down the bowl once or twice as necessary.

5. With clean beaters and using a clean mixing bowl, whip the egg whites on medium speed until frothy. Add the cream of tartar and continue to beat on medium speed until the egg whites begin to turn white. With the mixer still on medium speed, pour in the remaining ½ cup sugar in a slow, steady stream and whip until the whites hold stiff peaks.

6. Fold ¼ of the yolk mixture into the whites to lighten. Then fold the whites into the yolk mixture, gently but thoroughly. Pour the batter into the tube pan and

smooth the top with a rubber spatula. Bake the cake until it is golden brown and the top springs back when you touch it, 55 minutes to 1 hour.

7. Remove the pan from the oven. If your pan has feet, invert the pan onto a heatproof surface and allow it to cool. If your pan doesn't have feet, invert 4 heatproof drinking glasses on the counter and rest the inverted pan on top of the glasses to allow air to circulate around the cake while it cools. Let the cake cool in the pan completely, about 2 hours.

8. To remove the cake from the pan, run a sharp paring knife around the edges, being careful to leave the golden crust intact. Remove the sides of the pan. Invert the cake onto a serving platter. Run the paring knife under the removable bottom of the pan and lift it off the cake. Slice and serve.

9. Store uneaten cake in a cake keeper or wrap in plastic and store at room temperature for up to 3 days.

1 1/3 cups cake flour

2 teaspoons baking powder

1/2 teaspoon salt

1/2 cup mashed ripe bananas (from about 2 small bananas)

1/4 cup water

7 large eggs, 5 separated, 2 left whole

1 1/2 cups sugar

1/2 cup vegetable oil

1 teaspoon pure vanilla extract

1/2 cup finely chopped macadamia nuts

1/4 teaspoon cream of tartar

Banana–Macadamia Nut Chiffon Cake

SOMETIMES I KEEP BANANAS around too long (not hard). That's when they're ready to be baked into a cake like this one, a light and fluffy chiffon cake enriched with chopped macadamia nuts and mashed ripe bananas. I like it plain, but it is also great drizzled with the chocolate glaze (page 130) without the chopped Butterfinger bar.

1. Preheat the oven to 325°F. Have ready a 9-inch ungreased angel food tube pan with a removable bottom.

2. Combine the flour, baking powder, and salt in a medium bowl and whisk thoroughly to break up any lumps. Set aside. Combine the bananas and water in a small bowl. Set aside.

3. Place the egg yolks and whole eggs in a large mixing bowl and beat on medium-high speed until lightened in color, about 3 minutes. With the mixer running, add 1 cup sugar in a slow, steady stream and continue to beat until the mixture is light and increased in volume, about 5 minutes longer. With the mixer still running, slowly pour in the oil and continue to beat for 1 minute longer. Stir in the vanilla.

4. With the mixer on low speed, add 1/3 of the flour mixture, then 1/2 the banana and water mixture. Repeat with the remaining flour mixture and banana mixture, ending with the flour. Stir in the nuts.

5. With clean beaters and using a clean mixing bowl, whip the egg whites on medium speed until frothy. Add the cream of tartar and continue to beat on medium speed until the egg whites begin to turn white. With the mixer still on medium speed, pour in the remaining 1/2 cup sugar in a slow, steady stream and whip until the whites hold stiff peaks.

6. Fold 1/4 of the yolk mixture into the whites to lighten. Then fold the whites into the yolk mixture, gently but thoroughly. Pour the batter into the tube pan and smooth the top with a rubber spatula. Bake the cake until it is golden brown and the top springs back when you touch it, 55 minutes to 1 hour.

7. Remove the pan from the oven. If your pan has feet, invert the pan onto a heatproof surface and allow it to cool. If your pan doesn't have feet, invert 4 heatproof drinking glasses on the counter and rest the inverted pan on top of the glasses to allow air to circulate around the cake while it cools. Let the cake cool in the pan completely, about 2 hours.

8. To remove the cake from the pan, run a sharp paring knife around the edges, being careful to leave the golden crust intact. Remove the sides of the pan. Invert the cake onto a serving platter. Run the paring knife under the removable bottom of the pan and lift it off the cake. Slice and serve.

9. Store uneaten cake in a cake keeper or wrap in plastic and store at room temperature for up to 3 days.

2 tablespoons
plus 2 teaspoons
unsweetened Dutch
process cocoa powder

2 tablespoons water

1 1/2 cups plus
1 tablespoon sugar

1/2 cup plus 1 tablespoon
vegetable oil

1 1/3 cups cake flour

2 teaspoons baking
powder

1/2 teaspoon salt

7 large eggs,
5 separated, 2 left
whole

1 teaspoon pure vanilla
extract

1/4 teaspoon
cream of tartar

Chocolate Marble Chiffon Cake

OF THE HUNDRED CAKES in this book, this is my older daughter Rose's favorite one. Not only does it combine chocolate and vanilla, the flavor choices of every picky child, but it is so light that she can actually eat a whole piece before she is filled up.

1. Preheat the oven to 325°F. Have ready a 9-inch ungreased angel food tube pan with a removable bottom.

2. Whisk together the cocoa powder, water, 1 tablespoon sugar, and 1 tablespoon oil in a small bowl. Set aside. Combine the flour, baking powder, and salt in a medium bowl and whisk thoroughly to break up any lumps. Set aside.

3. Place the egg yolks and whole eggs in a large mixing bowl and beat on medium-high speed until lightened in color, about 3 minutes. With the mixer running, add 1 cup sugar in a slow, steady stream and continue to beat until the mixture is light and increased in volume, about 5 minutes longer. With the mixer still running, slowly pour in the remaining 1/2 cup oil and continue to beat for 1 minute longer.

4. With the mixer on low speed, add 1/3 of the flour mixture, then 1/2 the water mixture, then another 1/3 of the flour, the remaining water mixture, and the remaining flour mixture, scraping down the bowl once or twice as necessary. Stir in the vanilla.

5. With clean beaters and using a clean mixing bowl, whip the egg whites on medium speed until frothy. Add the cream of tartar and continue to beat on medium speed until the egg whites begin to turn white. With the mixer still on medium speed, pour in the remaining 1/2 cup sugar in a slow, steady stream and whip until the whites hold stiff peaks.

6. Fold 1/4 of the yolk mixture into the whites to lighten. Then fold the remaining whites into the yolk mixture, gently but thoroughly.

7. Transfer 1/3 of the cake batter to another bowl and gently fold in the chocolate batter. Pour half of the yellow batter into the tube pan. Top with half of the

continued on page 170

continued from page 168

chocolate batter. Repeat with the remaining yellow and chocolate batter. Smooth the top with a rubber spatula. Use a butter knife to swirl the batters together, taking care not to overmix. Bake the cake until it is golden brown and the top springs back when you touch it, 55 minutes to 1 hour.

8. Remove the pan from the oven. If your pan has feet, invert the pan onto a heatproof surface and allow it to cool. If your pan doesn't have feet, invert 4 heatproof drinking glasses on the counter and rest the inverted pan on top of the glasses to allow air to circulate around the cake while it cools. Let the cake cool in the pan completely, about 2 hours.

9. To remove the cake from the pan, run a sharp paring knife around the edges, being careful to leave the golden crust intact. Remove the sides of the pan. Invert the cake onto a serving platter. Run the paring knife under the removable bottom of the pan and lift it off the cake. Slice and serve.

10. Store uneaten cake in a cake keeper or wrap in plastic and store at room temperature for up to 3 days.

Index